Pilgrim's Progress Revisited

The Nonconformists of Banburyshire, 1662-2012

John Bunyan, author of Pilgrim's Progress, by Robert White, c.1679.

Pilgrim's Progress Revisited

The Nonconformists of Banburyshire
1662-2012

Martin Greenwood

THE WYCHWOOD PRESS

Our books may be ordered from your local bookshop or (post free) from
Evenlode Books, Market Street, Charlbury, OX7 3PH
01608 819117
e-mail: orders@evenlodebooks.co.uk

First published in 2013 by
The Wychwood Press, Alder House, Market Street, Charlbury OX7 3PH

The right of Martin Greeenwood to be identified as author of this work has been
asserted in accordance with the Copyright, Designs and Patents Act 1988

ISBN 978 1 902279 49 7

Printed in England by CPI Antony Rowe, Chippenham

Then said Evangelist, "Do you see yonder Wicket-Gate?"
The man said, "No."
Then said the other, "Do you see yonder shining light?"
He said, "I think I do."
Then said Evangelist, "Keep that light in your eye, and go directly thereto, so shalt thou see the Gate; at which, when thou knockest, it shall be told thee what thou shalt do."

Who would true valour see,
Let him come hither,
One here will constant be,
Come wind, come weather,
There's no discouragement
Shall make him once relent
His first avowed intent
To be a pilgrim.

JOHN BUNYAN

Contents

Tables

Illustrations

Colour photographs and illustrations

Notes on usage

Chapel/church/meeting-house: Common usage has been followed. Methodists have had smaller chapels and larger churches (and still do). Baptists have referred to both chapels and meeting-houses, while Quakers have had only meeting-houses. Anglicans have always gone to church, although they have also had some subsidiary chapelries.

Dissent / Nonconformity: Dissent is found more frequently in earlier periods. In the later nineteenth century, Nonconformity (with the same intended meaning) became more widely used. I have therefore used both terms in the book to describe Protestant denominations that became, or remained, separate from the Church of England.

Recusant: One who declined to attend the parish church. After 1570 the term usually applied to Roman Catholics.

Peculiar. A parish or church exempt from the jurisdiction of the archdeacon or bishop in whose diocese it lay. Usually it derived from the possession of land by a church dignitary lying within the diocese of another bishop. This applied to Banbury.

Tables:

(a) Chapelries, hamlets and townships are placed within their parishes.

(b) ave = average attendance at services.

(c) SS =- Sunday Scholars, i.e. children.

(d) N = Northamptonshire, W = Warwickshire.

Foreword and acknowledgements

'Hobgoblin nor foul fiend can daunt his spirit' John Bunyan

ON 7 FEBRUARY 2012 MY WIFE AND I attended an historic service at Westminster Abbey, which was held by the Church of England and the United Reformed Church to mark a significant step forward in the development of a shared relationship. The timing was significant, as this is the 350th anniversary year of the Act of Uniformity of 1662 and the Great Ejection of almost two thousand dissenting Presbyterian, Congregational and Baptist ministers from their livings. It is also the 40th anniversary of the inauguration of the United Reformed Church (URC), formed in 1972 when the Congregational Church in England and Wales and the Presbyterian Church of England came together. In broad terms, most of the ministers ejected in 1662 were Puritans, who now had to choose between conformity with the Church of England and Dissent. This was a defining moment, which could be said to have 'put an end to the Puritan dream of reforming the Church of England'.[1] A series of Acts, including the Act of Uniformity, which came to be called the Clarendon Code, brought persecution and suffering to those outside the established church. However, it may also be said to have laid the foundation of English Nonconformity; hence the significance of the special service at Westminster Abbey.

This is also a timely moment to remember John Bunyan (1628-88), whose spirit was certainly not daunted by the persecution which he had to suffer as a Dissenter after the Great Ejection. I have early memories of singing his great hymn 'Who would true valour see', particularly the verse with the hobgoblin. Sadly, the modern paler version has removed all reference to goblins and is all the weaker for it; it is nice to discover that the Methodists still sing the original version. I also remember having his *Pilgrim's Progress* read to me, and enjoying the rich cast of characters, like Faithful, Money-Love and Worldly Wiseman, and places like the Slough of Despond and Doubting Castle kept by Giant Despair. Bunyan wrote it during the twelve years which he spent in gaol for his religious convictions as a Dissenter (1660-72). The book was published in two parts (in 1678 and 1684) and by 1692 there were more than 100,000 copies in print in English alone. 'For many generations, *Pilgrim's Progress* was, after the Bible, the most deeply cherished book in the English-speaking household'.[2] It was often referred to as the 'lay bible'.

As we commemorate the 350th anniversary of the Act of Uniformity and the Great Ejection of Dissenting ministers, it seems appropriate to remember Bunyan's 'lay bible'. It is among the greatest books in the English language, 'translated into 200 languages and, next to the Bible, perhaps the world's best-selling book, especially in the Third World'.[3] It is a nice coincidence that we have just celebrated the 400th anniversary of the King James Bible, that other great religious book of the seventeenth century. *Pilgrim's Progress* and Bunyan's own life provide both the inspiration and the perfect starting point for writing about the Dissenters, or Nonconformists as they were called later in the nineteenth century. It has been fascinating to examine the progress of a great variety of local Dissenters from 1662 to the present day. I have to admit that I have not attempted to understand all the finer points of their religious differences, which are sometimes far from obvious; I am happy to leave them to others more qualified. This book is a possibly ambitious attempt to provide an overview of Dissent and Nonconformity in the Banburyshire region over the last 350 years.

Further inspiration has come from leading historical village walks in the Banburyshire region over the last fifteen years or more. During my walks I have always been impressed by the number and variety of Nonconformist chapels and meeting-houses. Although most of them are now closed and converted to private dwellings, a declining number do remain active. It therefore seems a timely moment not only to examine the history of Dissent and Nonconformity in the region but also to see what elements survive and what variety is still on offer. Although my prime interest is in the local villages, it is vital to include Banbury itself, which always seems to have been somehow separate and different from other towns and a stronghold of Nonconformity. It also continues to be a hub for its hinterland of villages, as it was in the nineteenth century. I have returned to look at the chapels and meeting-houses, their origins and some of the characters involved in their establishment. I have also tried to examine the interaction between the various dissenting groups where they were active in the same village and their relationship with the Church of England.

In the Introduction, I explain my use of the term 'Banburyshire', and why Dissent, or Nonconformity, has been so strong in the region. I look at how

Banbury's influence has transcended county boundaries, in the same way that they have little relevance in dealing with Nonconformity. In Chapter 1, I look at the Great Ejection of ministers in 1662, and the main sects or groups of Old Dissent which survived persecution under Charles II. I also look at John Bunyan's experience as a leading Dissenter and gifted preacher. In Chapter 2, I examine the results of the 1851 Religious Census, which provides an excellent guide to the parishes which have had Nonconformist chapels and meetings. In Chapter 3, I look at the history of the Methodists, or New Dissent, which has been complicated by a series of splinter groups. Most of them have had no impact locally, so that I have been able to concentrate my research on the main strands of Methodism: the Wesleyans, the Primitive Methodists, and to a lesser extent, Wesleyan Reform. This reveals the extent to which they have dominated Nonconformity in the region. I also take a look at the role and influence of the Methodists on village life, with particular emphasis on Fritwell, where they have played a very significant role, notably in the nineteenth century. I examine some of the leading characters, the trades and occupations of the local congregation, and the influence of the chapel on the local community.

In Chapters 4 to 6, I look at the history of the other main Nonconformist sects with a local presence: Baptists, Congregationalists or Independents, and Quakers. I have included the Presbyterians with the Congregationalists, since most of the orthodox Presbyterians came to describe themselves as Congregationalists, while the remainder eventually merged with them in 1972 in the United Reformed Church. In Chapter 7, I look at the history of the local Roman Catholics. Although they cannot strictly be described as Dissenters, they did decline to attend the parish church, like many Dissenters, and they had been called 'recusants' since the sixteenth century. In Chapter 8, on Chapel and Community, I look at the building of the chapels and meeting-houses, the social distinctions between the various Nonconformists, the relationship between the various sects, and their relations with the Church of England. In Chapter 9, I examine some other groups and movements with links to Nonconformity, including the Unitarians, the Salvation Army and the Temperance Movement.

I am extremely grateful to all those who have helped me in my research for this book, including Dot Dunkley (Syresham), Margaret Gibbs (Tysoe), Cheryl Messer (nee Gilkes) (Banbury), Geoffrey Keen and Don Walker (Fritwell), Walter Stageman (Greatworth), many Nonconformists of different persuasions and members of many local history societies. I would like to thank the staff at Banburyshire Studies, the Northamptonshire Record Office

(NRO), the Warwickshire Record Office (WRO), and Regent's Park College, Oxford. I would also like to thank the staff at the Oxford History Centre (OHC) for their patience and assistance in answering my queries and allowing me to use some photographs from the collections of the Oxfordshire County Council Photographic Archive (OCC). I must thank the Trustees of the British Museum for the image of John Bunyan, the Religious Society of Friends in Britain for the images of George Fox, the Trustees of Wesley's Chapel for the image of John Wesley, the National Portrait Gallery for the image of Cardinal Newman, and Regent's Park College, Oxford for the images of Charles Spurgeon.

I should add that my researches have allowed me to pursue my own pilgrimages to some key places in the history of Nonconformity, including the Bunyan Free Meeting Church and Museum in Bedford, John Wesley's birthplace in Epworth, Lincolnshire, and his City Road Church in London, and Charles Spurgeon's Metropolitan Tabernacle in the Elephant and Castle. I am very grateful to the staff in all those places for their generous assistance. I am extremely grateful to the Trustees of the Greening Lamborn Trust for their generous grant towards the cost of reproducing the illustrations. The Trust's objective is to promote public interest in the history, architecture, old photographs and heraldry of Oxford and its neighbourhood by supporting publications and other media that creates access to them.

I am very grateful to Julie Barrett for her map of Banburyshire and to Robin and Hazel Stagg (a local Methodist preacher) for their beautiful drawings of Methodist chapels. I am particularly grateful to Peter Silver for his skilled work in scanning and assembling all the photographs and illustrations for publication. I would like to thank James Nash for his rigorous reading of the text and his suggestions for improvement. I am hugely indebted to Jon Carpenter for agreeing to publish this book and for his help and encouragement along the way. Finally I must thank my wife, Anne, for her patience while I have been tracking down all the chapels and wrestling all the data into book form; without her support this book would never have been written. Finally, I can only hope that this overview of the wide variety of Nonconformist groups in Banburyshire over the centuries tells an interesting and possibly inspiring story. I have certainly found it so.

Martin Greenwood
Fringford, January 2013

Introduction

Why Banburyshire?

'THE TERM 'BANBURYSHIRE', MUCH USED IN THE 1830S, was not just an affectation, for Banbury's economy was in many respects comparable with that of most county towns'.[1]

This is not a book about North Oxfordshire or South Northamptonshire or South Warwickshire, it is about parts of all three of them. Although the term 'Banburyshire' was not familiar until the late eighteenth and early nineteenth centuries, it could have been used much earlier to describe a distinct region. Even in prehistoric and Roman times there was 'an intensive network of trackways' in the Banbury district, including the Jurassic Way that connected Bath with Lincoln and the Port Way that intersected on a north to south alignment. Indeed 'the frame of the area is set by a great triangle of Roman roads comprising the Fosse Way, Watling Street and Akeman Street'.[2] On the religious front, the Diocese of Oxford was created in 1542. However, the Dean and Chapter of Lincoln continued to exercise jurisdiction over the Peculiar of Banbury: that is for Banbury, Cropredy (which included Great and Little Bourton), Claydon, Mollington and Wardington, and Horley and Hornton in Oxfordshire and King's Sutton in Northamptonshire. This arrangement continued until 1858. It was not until 1889 that changes to county boundaries brought all the parish of Banbury into Oxfordshire. This is a further indication of the separate nature of the Banbury region.

The only known political definition of the area came in 1834, when the Poor Law Amendment Act was passed and parishes were actively encouraged or coerced into unions; this made the provision of large workhouse buildings viable. As part of this process, a new Banbury Poor Law Union was established, representing the greater part of the Banbury Region. In addition to the Banbury borough, the new Union consisted of 50 other parishes, 35 in Oxfordshire, eight in Northamptonshire and seven in Warwickshire. In 1843 the extent of Banbury's hinterland and influence was well defined by the editor of the *Banbury Guardian*: 'To the 140 places within a circuit of ten miles it may be said to be a metropolis'.[3] In fact the routes of the country carriers into Banbury show that its influence extended well beyond the ten-mile circuit and there were many travelling some 15-20 miles for the Thursday Market Day.

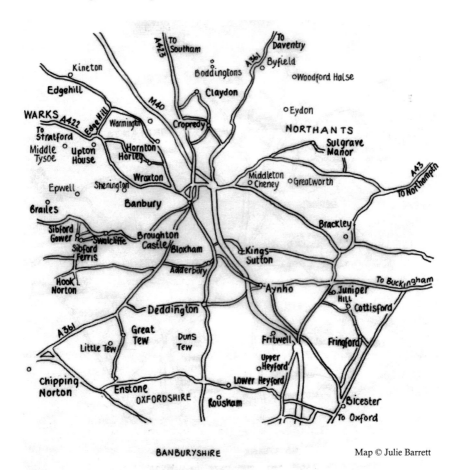

BANBURYSHIRE

Map © Julie Barrett

Banbury had many more carriers' services than county towns like Oxford, Newcastle and Shrewsbury, and only a few less than Nottingham, Leicester and Reading. These carriers' visits transcended county boundaries, coming in from the Four Shires: Buckinghamshire, Northamptonshire and Warwickshire, as well as Oxfordshire. In 1860, the *Banbury Advertiser* asked 'Is any other little town so visited?'

This all shows how Banbury's status has been more like that of a county town than just a successful market town. Indeed, its influence on the region has continued to the present day. Notably, it was the largest stock-market in Europe from the 1960s until trading ceased in 1998, and its influence has been revived by the opening of the M40 motorway in 1991. This has made Banbury an ideal business centre and one of the lowest areas for unemployment in the whole country. 'The second largest town in the county has always been conscious of its individuality and has never lost an opportunity to express it'.[4]

Geographically, much of the region is the 'Red Lands', where local quarries have produced the golden brown stone used so extensively in Banbury and the neighbouring villages. There are also some obvious boundaries to the region. To the south, the Buckingham-Aynho-Deddington road was the ancient boundary between Wessex and Mercia; and to the east, Brackley is a natural limit. To the west, the villages of Swerford, Hook Norton, and the Sibfords are also a natural limit, while Chipping Norton is clearly more a part of the Cotswolds. To the north, the Edgehill escarpment is a natural boundary, but Banbury's influence has often stretched well beyond it to the Kineton area. In the same way, county boundaries are of little relevance when looking at Nonconformity in the region. The Banbury Methodist Circuit, in particular, has always included a number of meetings and chapels in South Northamptonshire and South Warwickshire.

The region has been a stronghold of Dissent over a long period. This can be explained, at least in part, by the remoteness of many of the local villages. They have been well away from any main route and most of them have been what is called 'open' rather than 'closed'. A 'closed' village may be described as one where a squire or absentee landlord was in control by owning at least half the acreage e.g. Great Tew and Heythrop, while an 'open' village would have had many small proprietors with no overall control e.g. Cropredy and Hornton. This is not an absolute distinction and there are obviously many other factors and intermediate cases. One common characteristic of these 'open' villages has been Dissent, and Banburyshire has been a stronghold for Dissenters since the Civil War. It was also a natural recruiting ground for the Methodists in the eighteenth and nineteenth centuries. Banbury itself has been notable for its variety of Dissenting denominations, particularly in the nineteenth century, and there is still considerable variety. I am well aware that there are conflicting views about the use of the term Banburyshire. However, in writing about the Nonconformists of the region, the inclusive term seems to provide the perfect solution. It is time to look at the origins of Old Dissent in the seventeenth century and the effects of the Great Ejection of 1662.

Chapter 1

Old Dissent

'The World turn'd upside down', 1640-60

IN 1646, AT THE END OF THE FIRST CIVIL WAR, a well-known tract was published under the title *The World turn'd upside down*, by T.J., a well-wisher to King, Parliament and Kingdom (pictured). It seems a fair description of the whole period of the Civil War and the Interregnum from 1640 to 1660. It was a time of turbulence and hardship for much of the country, unlike anything seen before or since. The countryside surrounding Banbury, stretching well into Warwickshire and Northamptonshire, became a militarised buffer zone between the Royalists and the Parliamentarians. The region witnessed the destructive sieges of Banbury, the Battle of Edgehill and numerous smaller skirmishes at Cropredy, Compton Wynyates and elsewhere. It is unlikely, therefore, that any local villages escaped the impact of the Civil War. The region was on the main Royalist supply route for men and arms from the north-west to Oxford, and the Parliamentarian route from London to their strongholds in Coventry and Warwick.

Apart from the main protagonists, a variety of rebellious splinter groups appeared and contributed to what today we might call a 'broken society'. Groups like the Diggers and the Levellers were fighting for their rights to land, greater equality

Holy Trinity Chapel, Staunton Harold. The pulpit erected in 1662.
© National Trust

'The World turn'd upside down, from Civil War tract, 1646.

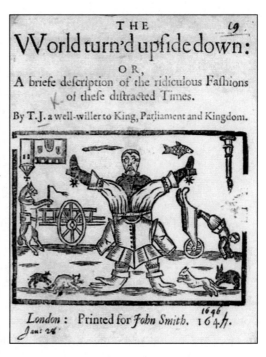

THE
World turn'd upfide down:
OR,

A briefe defcription of the ridiculous Fafhions of thefe diftracted Times.

By T.J. a well-willer to King, Parliament and Kingdom.

London : Printed for *John Smith*. 1647.

and for social change. On the religious front, the King and Archbishop Laud both went to the scaffold, churches were vandalised, and in 1647 the Presbyterian Church was made the official church of the country. At the same time, a great variety of new religious sects appeared on the scene, including the Quakers and other lesser-known ones like the Seekers and Muggletonians.

This made it a difficult time for Church of England ministers, with many of them suffering hardship and forced to leave their livings. In Leicestershire, the Chapel of the Holy Trinity in Staunton Harold (Plate 2) stands as a unique and beautiful memorial to this unsettled period for loyal Anglicans.[1] It should be said that the sublime beauty of both the chapel and its setting has to be seen to be believed. The young Royalist squire, Sir Robert Shirley, defied the Puritan regime in 1653 by building this private chapel for Staunton Harold Hall. It 'expressed the purest Anglicanism', for which Archbishop Laud had striven and died on the scaffold. It included an altar, then strictly forbidden, and some unique paintings of the Creation on the ceiling, which were also likely to give offence to the Puritans. The chapel is not quite the only one built or rebuilt during the Interregnum. 'But as an example of High Church architecture planned and built in defiance of the Puritan regime, the chapel is unique'.[2] Sadly Shirley never saw it completed. Cromwell on hearing of his fine chapel is reported to have asked why he could not pay towards a ship for the navy when he could afford so fine a building. When he refused, he was arrested and imprisoned in the Tower, where he died in 1656 aged 27, probably of gaol fever. The finishing touches to the chapel were carried out in 1662-5. The inscription above the west entrance of the church seems to sum up 'The World turn'd upside down' and 'may serve as an epigraph on Royalism in eclipse':

In the yeare 1653
when all things Sacred were throughout ye nation,
Either demolisht or profaned
Sir Robert Shirley, Barronet,
Founded this church;
Whose singular praise it is
to have done the best things in ye worst times,
and
hoped them in the most callamitous.
The righteous shall be had in everlasting remembrance.

Shirley would have shared some of the views which Sir John Oglander, a Royalist squire, expressed in his commonplace notebook about the social changes of the 1640s. His views may be over stated but here are some examples: 'Gentlemen could call nothing their own and lived in slavery and submission to the unruly, base multitude.. We had a thing called a Committee, which over-ruled Deputy Lieutenants and also Justices of the Peace'. The Committee included a pedlar, apothecary, baker and farmers and 'these ruled the whole Island'.[3] These views reflect the assumption that it was the gentry's right to rule. Within a decade, the world was turned upside down again and the gentry and Anglican ministers resumed their natural place in society. It was now the turn of Puritan ministers to suffer hardship and ejection from their livings. The Restoration of Charles II would bring the persecution of Old Dissent but also the creation of English Nonconformity.

The Persecution of Dissent, 1660-1689[4]

This period is mainly the story of two of the greatest figures in the history of English Dissent: John Bunyan (1628-88), the author of *Pilgrim's Progress*, and George Fox (1624-91) (pictured), the founder of the Quaker Movement. Bunyan may never have preached in Oxfordshire but his great allegory would have been very familiar locally, as it has been a best seller to many denominations all round the world. Fox, however, made many visits to the region and in 1675 he formally opened the meeting-house in Adderbury. He was also the inspiration for the meeting-house in Sibford Gower. The Civil War had seen the birth of a great variety of new religious sects but it was only the Quakers, led by Fox, who found lasting support and survived in any strength. There were others whose origins can be traced back before the Civil War - the Independents, or Congregationalists, and the General and Particular Baptists.

There were also the Presbyterians, who were not a sect at all, and whose church had been officially adopted in Scotland in 1560. It had much influence in early seventeenth-century England and in 1647 it was made the official church of the country.

It is a tribute to the organizing genius of Fox that the Quakers were able to survive the turmoil of the Interregnum and the persecution after the Restoration. It was also because of the nature of his message, which he claimed was a direct revelation from God and which struck a chord with many Friends. For five years from 1648 he travelled round the north Midlands and Yorkshire gathering 'divers meetings of Friends'. He was helped by his powerful voice, which caused one judge before whom he appeared to complain that 'thou speakest so loud, thy voice drowns mine and the court's'.[5] His breakthrough, which led to the expansion of Quakerism, came in 1652, when he spoke on Pendle Hill in Lancashire and later to a thousand people on Firbank Fell, near Kendal. Although Fox spent time in gaol in the 1650s, the persecution of the Quakers during the Interregnum was localised and spasmodic after 1652, and they were largely unmolested in their northern strongholds and in London and Bristol.

The Restoration brought major changes, with the Cavalier Parliament determined to strengthen the Church of England and encourage religious conformity. This brought persecution of the Dissenters, particularly the Quakers, under a series of Acts, usually known together as the Clarendon Code, and including the Act of Uniformity of 1662. The Act required all ministers and schoolmasters to give their 'unfeigned assent and consent' to the Book of Common Prayer of the Church of England by the Feast of St Bartholomew, 24 August 1662. This Prayer Book was so new that most had never even seen a copy. In addition, episcopal ordination was required for all ministers. As a result, nearly 1,000 clergy gave up their livings, and, in what became known as the Great Ejection (or Ejectment), a total of 2,029 clergy, lecturers, and fellows refused to comply and were deprived of their livings between 1660 and 1662. The figure for England was 1,909, with a further 120 in Wales.[6] Table 1 provides the best estimates of the number ejected for the three local counties,

GEO. FOX

George Fox, woodcut found in the 1694 edition of Fox's journal. © Religious Society of Friends in Britain.

Table 1		Number of Dissenting Ministers Ejected, 1660-1662			
County	Totals	Ejected 1660	Ejected 1662	Ejected Date Uncertain	Afterwards Conform'd
Oxfordshire	23	13	10	0	4
Northamptonshire	46	14	31	1	7
Warwickshire	31	6	22	3	2
Highest Numbers					
Devon	121	40	73	8	10
Yorkshire	110	38	52	20	17
England	1,909	812	968	129	177

compared to the highest numbers elsewhere and to England as a whole. The low figures for Oxfordshire are not surprising, given the strong Anglican tradition in most of the county and natural opposition to any Dissent. It should be noted that 220 of those ejected were lecturers, assistants and curates serving chapels of ease, some 355 may not be valid ejections, and more may have afterwards conformed.

The ministers left their livings (apart from some who later conformed) and joined those Congregational and Baptist ministers already serving outside the Established Church. This significantly increased the ministerial strength of Dissent after the Great Ejection, and successive generations of Dissenters always remembered 'Black Bartholomew's Day'. At the same time Presbyterianism was overthrown as the official religion of the country. As a result, the Clarendon Code can be said to have created English Nonconformity, and it may be seen 'as a step towards the eventual and permanent liberation of Dissent'.[7]

The main survivors of persecution under the Clarendon Code were the Presbyterians, Independents, Baptists and Quakers. These groups are normally described as Dissenters, at least until the latter part of the nineteenth century when Nonconformists became the more usual term. The boundaries between these different denominations were sometimes indistinct and even in the eighteenth century it was not always easy to classify ministers. John Bunyan was a case in point, since he was very reluctant to be pigeon-holed either as a Baptist or an Independent. The severity of the persecution of Dissenters varied and there were also geographical variations, with Oxfordshire said to be 'the persecuted shire of England'.[8] The definition of a Dissenter, however, was not always easy, as some of them attended conventicles (illegal meetings) as well as the parish church. The Church itself also needed to improve, its cause not helped by plurality (priests holding a number of benefices), the absence of curates, and the poor pay for priests.

In 1676 Bishop Compton of London, acting on the instructions of Archbishop Sheldon, requested the bishops to obtain from their clergy an estimate of the 'number of persons, or at least families, residing within their parishes, and of the number of Dissenters 'who either obstinately refuse, or wholly absent themselves from the communion of the Church of England'. This census, however, is of limited use as an indication of the size and distribution of the Dissenting community. The Archbishop failed to make clear whether the clergy should count persons or families, and they were not asked to give the denomination of the Dissenters. Although the census only gives the statistical breakdown between Papists and Nonconformists, it does provide an indication of the places in Banburyshire where the number of Nonconformists was highest. These included Bloxham and Milcombe (100), Hook Norton (90), Great and Little Tew (43), Adderbury and Milton (40), Deddington (35), and South Newington (30). We shall see below that these villages still had high numbers of Nonconformists in the nineteenth century. The 90 Nonconformists recorded in Hook Norton represented over 20% of the population, a startling number; it is likely that some two thirds of them were Baptists, many of them Anabaptists. Their treatment is a good example of local persecution. In 1664 two leading Baptists were arrested and jailed in Oxford. In 1665 the Church excommunicated sixteen from the village and in 1682 the curate was suspended by the Bishop of Oxford because of the level of Dissent. In 1684 a further twenty-eight were suspended.

The position of the Roman Catholics was different. They were an established church, like the Presbyterians, and not strictly one of the Dissenting sects. However, like the Dissenters, they had been regarded as 'recusants', those who refused to attend their parish church, since the sixteenth century. After the Restoration they must have hoped for toleration, as Charles was thought to be a secret Catholic and have some sympathy for them. However, the Cavalier Parliament certainly did not share either his desire for religious toleration or his sympathy with Roman Catholicism. The Catholics, therefore, do have a place in any study of Dissent in the Banburyshire region. In general, Dissenters worshipped more freely in towns, although their plea of 'conscience' irritated the Anglican ministers, who said that they needed to 'get the conscience rightly employed'.

The greatest sufferers were the Quakers, because they refused to accept many of the doctrines and rituals of the established church. They insisted that there was no reason why they should remove their hats in Church, and they refused to swear an oath in court or pay tithes. Not surprisingly, magistrates resented them and their enthusiastic and outspoken defence of their beliefs, which they saw as subversive behaviour. 'Enthusiasm' of this kind was seen as subversive and unacceptable, as it was later from the Methodists. Fox himself spent three years in Lancaster gaol and Scarborough Castle from 1663 to 1666 and was only freed on the orders of Charles II. The King intervened on a number of occasions to save Dissenters from the consequences of the penal code. Most importantly, he introduced the Declaration of Indulgence in 1672, which suspended 'all manner of penal laws in matters ecclesiastical'. Some 491 Dissenters were pardoned, most of them Friends. 'Henceforward Dissenters would be able to meet freely for worship provided that they had a licence for their meeting and for their preacher'.[9] This provided an important stimulus to Dissent but it was alarming to members of the Established Church.

Bunyan, who was one of those freed in 1672, epitomises the remarkable enthusiasm and endurance of these early Dissenters in their struggle for religious freedom. He was born near Bedford and served in the Parliamentary army during the Civil War. In spite of his humble origins as a tinker, he became known as a gifted preacher in the 1650s and after the Restoration he was sent to gaol for his religious convictions as a Dissenter. He refused to give an assurance not to preach, and remained in the County Gaol for twelve years. On his release in 1672, he became pastor of the Bedford Congregational church. He had written *Pilgrim's Progress* by then but publication was delayed until 1678, because he was deterred by some of his friends' negative reaction to the allegory. Part 1 was published in 1678 and Part II in 1684. By 1692, just four years after his death, there were more than 100,000 copies in print in English alone. It was written amid bitter sectarian controversy but it has transcended religious rivalries and over the years it has appeared in Catholic, Anglo-Catholic and Unitarian versions. 'For many generations, *Pilgrim's Progress* was, after the Bible, the most deeply cherished book in the English-speaking household'.[10] This allegory of Christian's life as a journey from the City of Destruction to the Celestial City has appealed to millions over the ages, and, like Bunyan's life, it epitomises the struggles of the early Dissenters.

During the 1670s and 1680s his gifts as a preacher were recognised well beyond his native Bedfordshire. Although there is no record of him preaching in the Banbury area, he did preach to affiliated churches in Hertfordshire, Huntingdonshire and Cambridgeshire, as far as intermittent persecution allowed. He also had significant links with London, particularly with churches in Moorfields and Southwark. He almost certainly preached too at the

Independent Stepney church of Matthew Meade, a Bedfordshire man who had the largest congregation in London. Bunyan's reputation was sensational enough for Charles II to have heard of him and to ask John Owen about him. Owen had emerged, at mid-century, as the most influential Congregational minister in the country. He rose rapidly in Cromwell's favour, becoming dean of Christ Church, Oxford, in 1651, and, in 1652, vice-chancellor of the university. He survived the Restoration and earned the respect of Charles II, and his Moorfields church was attended by the Puritan aristocracy. When asked about Bunyan, he apparently told the King that he would gladly exchange his learning for the tinker's power in the pulpit.

Bunyan was impatient with arguments about the need for adult baptism and other forms and ceremonies and he rejected the label 'Baptist' (see Chapter 4). In 1672 the Bedford church took out its licence as 'Congregational' not 'Baptist', although other supposed Baptist churches did the same. Sectarian lines were not yet fully drawn and as late as 1766 the Bedford church still thought of itself as 'Independent'. When his new church was built in Bedford in 1850, it was called the Bunyan Meeting Free Church. Today it is a member of the Congregational Federation and the Baptist Union; it is also an observer at the United Reformed Church. I am sure that Bunyan would have approved this broad church view.

The Toleration of Dissent, 1690-1730

The Glorious Revolution of 1688 saw the expulsion of the Catholic James II and the arrival of the Protestant William and Mary from Holland. It also marked the end of what has been called 'the heroic age of Dissent. One by one their greatest leaders were passing from the stage'.[11] John Owen died in 1683, John Bunyan in 1688, and George Fox in 1691. In 1689 the Toleration Act finally allowed the Dissenters freedom of worship, provided that they took the oaths of allegiance and supremacy. This gave them the right to have their own places of worship together with teachers and preachers. They were still excluded from public office, although they were able to qualify for municipal office by 'occasional conformity' with Anglicanism. This provision was overturned by an Act of 1711, which was designed to prevent Dissenters from receiving communion in the Anglican church so as to qualify for civil or military office.

Perversely, as both Bunyan and Fox feared, the tolerance and prosperity, which followed the overthrow of James II in 1688, sapped the zeal of the Dissenters and led to a decline in their numbers by the second quarter of the

Table 2	Estimates of Dissenting Numbers in early 18th-Century Oxfordshire		
Denomination	No. of Congregations	Hearers	% of pop'n
Presbyterians	8	2,600	2.99
Independents	1	450	0.52
Particular Baptists	4	230	0.26
General Baptists	2	110	0.13
Quakers	14	780	0.90
	29	4,170	4.80

eighteenth century. Even by 1715, not much more than 6% of the population of England could be counted as Dissenters, some 338,000 out of a total population of 5.4 million. At this point the Presbyterians still dominated the scene with some 179,000 members or 3.3%.[12] There are two major surveys of the distribution of Old Dissent in the late seventeenth and early eighteenth centuries: the Compton Census of 1676, as we have seen, and the list of Dissenting congregations compiled by Dr John Evans, mainly between 1715 and 1718. There are also Bishop Secker's visitation returns of 1738, in which, for example, ten Oxfordshire clergymen reported that the number of Dissenters was 'of late years considerably decreased' and in Wroxton the Baptist meeting house had not been used for 15 years.[13]

Table 2 provides estimates of Dissenting Numbers in early 18th-century Oxfordshire,[14] when the estimated population of the county was 86,930. These estimates are based on the Evans list (1715-18), Bishop Secker's visitation returns (1738), baptismal registers, church membership lists, and Quaker burial registers.

The overall percentage of Dissenters in the county of 4.8% is even lower than the estimate of 6% in 1715. This confirms the decline in Dissenting numbers in early 18th-century Oxfordshire. Following this decline, however, there was an Evangelical revival in the late eighteenth and early nineteenth centuries. 'This brought a huge increase in the adherents to the Baptists and Congregationalists and ultimately added to them the biggest Nonconformist denomination of all: the Methodists'.[15] Before looking at the rise of Methodism, or New Dissent, it is time to examine the results of the 1851 Religious Census, which provides a perfect starting point for looking both forward and back at the number of Dissenters in the region.

Chapter 2

The 1851 Religious Census

'...ALMOST EVERY SECT IN BANBURY was represented, Unitarians, Methodists, of all shades, Congregationalists, Hyper-Calvinists, and church people. Coming up to the chapel in the conveyance, he (Charles Spurgeon) asked me what denominations we had in Banbury. I told him I thought we pretty well had them all. Indeed, it had been said that if a man lost his religion, he might well find it in Banbury'.[1]

In 1857, W.T. Henderson (1825-1911), the very successful Baptist minister at the Bridge Street Chapel, had invited the famous Baptist preacher, Charles Spurgeon, to visit Banbury. This is an excerpt from his diary describing the visit, and we shall have more to say about Spurgeon in Chapter 4. His comment about the variety of religious denominations available in Banbury in 1857 is relevant here, since it was written only a few years after the unique religious census of 1851. It gives some idea of the variety of Dissent available in the Banburyshire region, at a time when Dissenting numbers were at their peak.

On Sunday 30 March 1851, everyone attending a place of worship in England and Wales was counted, in order to provide a national census of accommodation and attendance at worship. A number of voices in the Church of England, including Bishop Wilberforce of Oxford, had advised against it, and he predicted, rightly as it transpired, that the census would be a disaster for the Church of England. The overall results for England and Wales showed that only some 50% of the population attended a service and, even worse, of them some 50% were Dissenters: thus only 25% of the population attended a Church of England service. In Oxfordshire, the Banbury Registration District had by far the largest percentage (44.29%) of Dissenter sittings. This contrasts with the figures for Oxfordshire as a whole, where Anglicanism was dominant as you would expect in a traditional agricultural county, with 67.2% of the sittings Anglican and only 32.8% Dissenting. Tables 3(a) and 3(b) show the 1851 Religious Census figures for Banburyshire for parishes with Nonconformist chapels, the former for parishes in Oxfordshire, the latter for ones in Northamptonshire and Warwickshire. I have shown the county break-down, although county boundaries have little significance when examining

Nonconformity in the region. This is particularly true of the Banbury Methodist Circuit, as we shall see in the next chapter. In the following tables, ave = average attendance and SS = Sunday Scholars (children).

Notes to Table 3(a)
Oxfordshire Parishes

   1. *Neithrop*
Christ Church Chapel, a former Presbyterian chapel, was now Unitarian.
   2. *Adderbury*
The parish consisted of the townships of Adderbury East and West, the chapelries of Barford St John and Bodicote, and the hamlet of Milton. The total population was 2,310.
   3. *Middle Barton*
A hamlet and township in Steeple Barton.
   4. *Bloxham*
The parish included the chapelry of Milcombe.
   5. *Broughton*
The parish included the hamlet of North Newington.
   6. *Cropredy*
The parish included the township of Great and Little Bourton, the chapelries of Claydon and Wardington, and part of the chapelry of Mollington. The total population was 2,602.
   7. *Mollington*
A chapelry lying partly in Cropredy parish and partly in Kineton Hundred, Warwickshire.
   8. *Deddington*
The parish included the hamlets of Clifton and Hempton.
   9. *Lower Heyford*
The parish included the hamlet of Caulcott.
   10. *South Newington*
Originally a Quaker meeting-house but in 1851 it was leased by the Methodists.
   11. *South Newington Parish Church*
'Numbers somewhat smaller than they were five years ago in consequence of 72 persons having emigrated to America'.
   12. *Swalcliffe*
The parish included the chapelries of Epwell and Shutford East, and the townships of Shutford West, Sibford Ferris and Sibford Gower. The total population was 2,012.

Table 3(a) Religious Census for Banburyshire, 30 March 1851
Nonconformist Chapels with their Parish Churches

Oxfordshire Parishes

Parish	Population 1851	Denomination	Services am/pm	Evening	Date
Banbury	8,793	Friends	60/39		1750
		Strict Baptist-WestSt	70	50	1829
		Independent	100	120	pre-1800
		Wesleyan	361/118 SS 197	470	1811
		Primitive Methodist (Broad St.)	72/123 SS 87/89	144	1839
		Bridge St.Baptist	150 SS 50	200	1841
		St.John's RC	250	230	1838
		Parish Church	1000-300 SS300/300	1,300	pre-1800
Neithrop (township)	4,180	Baptist	70 SS 39/37	77	1834
		Unitarian (Note 1)	124 SS 79	214	1850

Villages

Parish	Population 1851	Denomination	Services am/pm	Evening	Date
Adderbury East	978	Wesleyan (Note 2)	/23 SS 12/13	36	1810
		Parish Church	ave 240		pre-1800
Adderbury West	370	Independent	51 SS 20/19	120	1829
		Friends	16		1675
Bodicote	673	Baptist & Indep.	/50		1817-18
		Wesleyan	SS 54	60	1846
		Chapelry	156/190		1844
Milton (hamlet)	164	Primitive Methodist	/35 /SS 25	27	pre-1800
Barford St John	125	Chapelry	ave 15-20		
Barford St Michael	392	Baptist	ave 20		
		Wesleyan	40 SS 20	92 SS30	1840
		Parish Church	ave 80		
Barton (Middle)	hamlet	Wesleyan (Note 3)	181 SS 45/40	188	1831
Barton (Steeple)	757	Parish Church	94	136	pre-1800

Table 3(a) Religious Census for Banburyshire, 30 March 1851
continued   **Nonconformist Chapels with their Parish Churches**

Oxfordshire Parishes

Parish	Population 1851	Denomination	am/pm	Evening	Date
Barton	279	Primitive Methodist	/130	136	
(Westcott)		Parish Church	80/110		pre-1800
			SS 47/40		
Bloxham	1,336	Baptist	/75	100	1812
		Wesleyan	/126	120	1821
			/SS 27		
		Mother Church	250/250		c.1200
		(Note 4)	SS100/100		
Hethe	418	RC Chapel	150		1832
		Wesleyan	30/60	50	1814
			SS 25/30		
		Parish Church	70/100		pre-1800
			SS 30/30		
Heyford	605	Wesleyan	ave 50		1804
(Lower)		Parish Church	ave200/200		pre-1800
		(Note 9) SS	ave 50/50		
Caulcott		Wesleyan	/80	88	
Heyford	399	Wesleyan	22/92	101	pre-1800
(Upper)		Primitive Methodist	ave 40		1848
		Parish Church	92		
Heythrop	190	R.C. Church	63	14	pre-1800
		Parish Church	75		pre-1800
Hook	1,496	Primitive Methodist	60	100	1826
Norton		Wesleyan	/100	160	1813
			/SS 74		
		Baptist	100/120		1787
			SS 20/20		
		Friends	11		pre-1800
		Parish Church	160/277		pre-1800
			SS 92/98		
Horley	392	Wesleyan	75	90	pre-1800
		Primitive Methodist		40	
		Parish Church	/82		pre-1800
			SS 48		
Hornton	591	Primitive Methodist	102	140	1842
			SS 20/20		
		Independent	38		1834
		Parish Church	98		pre-1800
			SS 45		

Table 3(a) Religious Census for Banburyshire, 30 March 1851
continued Nonconformist Chapels with their Parish Churches

Oxfordshire Parishes

Parish	Population 1851	Denomination	am/pm	Evening	Date
Sheningt'n	437	Independent	ave 30 ave SS 20	ave 55	1817
		Primitive Methodist	80		c.1817
		Parish Church	c.100/c.90 SS 60/60		pre-1800
Souldern	619	Wesleyan	SS50	108	1850
		Parish Church	118/112 SS 36/37		
South Newington	419	Wesleyan (Note 10)		110	1692
		Parish Ch. (Note 11)	77/116 SS 50/50		pre-1800
Swalcliffe	367	Parish Ch. (Note 12)	130/132 SS 42/44		pre-1800
Epwell	330	Primitive Methodist.	/129 /SS 16	150	1830
		Chapelry	32 SS 36		pre-1800
Shutford	24	Chapelry	/45 /SS 26		pre-1800
West Shutford	392	Wesleyan	80 /SS 15	100 SS 12	1837
Sibford Gower (township)	549	Friends	112		pre-1800
		Wesleyan	100 /SS 30	90	1827
		Parish Church	ave320/400		1840
StokeLyne	631	Wesleyan	68		1838
		Parish Church	30		
Tew(Great)	541	Parish Church	135/119 SS 70/70		pre-1800
Tew(Little)	237	Baptist	117		1829
		Chapelry (Note 13)		75	
Wigginton	314	Particular Baptist		35	1835
		Parish Ch. (Note 14)	109/117		
Wroxton	789	Wesleyan (Note 15)	78	43	c.1820
		Independent		50-60	1826
		Parish Church	134 SS 49		pre-1800
Balscott		Wesleyan	/51	95	1850
		Chapelry	/64 /SS 21		pre-1800

13. *Little Tew*

A chapelry in Great Tew parish. Services were held in the National School House.

14. *Wigginton*

Attendance includes Sunday Scholars.

15. *Wroxton*

The parish included the chapelry of Balscott.

Table 3(b) shows the 1851 Religious Census figures for parishes with their Nonconformist chapels in the Northamptonshire and Warwickshire areas of Banburyshire.

Notes to Table 3(b)

Northamptonshire and Warwickshire Parishes

1. *Byfield*

'The undersigned (Curate) is not able to state the living of Byfield which is under sequestration, nor the number of sittings in the church.' Notes to the census indicate that the Revd Charles Wetherell, Rector 1819-67, was a scandalous clergyman.

2. *Eydon*

The chapel was for the 'United Brethren' commonly called 'Moravians'.

3. *Middleton Cheney*

The Baptist chapel was built in lieu of a former small place in another part of the village. Evening service was a public prayer meeting.

4. *Woodford Halse*

The chapel was for the 'United Brethren' commonly called 'Moravians'.

5. *Brailes*

a) The Wesleyans did not meet in a separate building. Later they met in the old Friends' meeting-house. Later still they built a chapel, which is now a private dwelling. Sometime after the Union in 1932, the Methodists all moved to the Primitive Methodist chapel.

b) The Primitive Methodists built a chapel in 1848; it only closed very recently.

c) The Quakers had no meeting on this day as they only met twelve times a year. Once a month they joined another meeting.

d) The Roman Catholics' average congregation was about 400, coming from sixteen parishes.

e) The Anglican congregation was smaller than usual in the morning, as there was a collection for the Propagation of the Gospel in Foreign Parts!

Table 3(b) Religious Census for Banburyshire, 30 March 1851
Nonconformist Chapels with their Parish Churches

Northamptonshire Parishes

Parish	Population 1851	Denomination	am/pm	Evening	Date
Boddingt'n (Lower)	327	Wesleyan	/50	57	1836
Boddingt'n (Upper)	399	Parish Church	100/190 SS 93/93		pre-1800
Byfield	1,021	Independent	100/130 SS 18/21	160	1827
		Primitive Methodist	50	100	1849
		Parish Ch. (Note 1)			pre-1800
Chacombe	506	Wesleyan	93	107	1816
		Primitive Methodist	ave 50		1851
		Parish Church	120/150 SS50/50		pre-1800
Chipping Warden	521	Wesleyan	86 /SS 23	81 SS13	c.1807
		Parish Church	93/141 SS 48/48		pre-1800
Eydon	621	Moravian (Note 2)	27	109	1818
		Quakers	13		pre-1800
		Parish Church	120/180 SS 63/63		pre-1800
F'thinghoe	416	Primitive Methodist	20	90	pre-1800
		Parish Church	190/248 SS 52/52		pre-1800
Greatw'rth	135	Wesleyan	80	80	1844
		Parish Church	51/81 SS 12/12		pre-1800
King's Sutton	1,335	Baptist	80	116	1826
		Wesleyan	15/53		c.1820
		Parish Church	380		pre-1800
Middleton Cheney	1,330	Baptist (Note 3)	70/130 SS 48/41	45 SS 32	1806
		Wesleyan	194/SS 48	265	1810
		Primitive Methodist	/100 /SS 63	110	1849
		Parish Church	40/120 SS 75/75		pre-1800
Sulgrave	604	Baptist	80/150 SS 30	100	1844
		Parish Church	101/164 SS 56/55		pre-1800

Table 3(b)   Religious Census for Banburyshire, 30 March 1851
continued   Nonconformist Chapels with their Parish Churches

Northamptonshire Parishes

Parish	Population 1851	Denomination	am/pm	Evening	Date
Syresham	1,027	Wesleyan	/166	183	1846
		Parish Church	100/261		pre-1800
			SS 57/69		
Whitfield	326	Wesleyan	/40	53	c.1823
		Parish Church	59/82		pre-1800
			SS 42/45		
Woodford Halse	800	Moravian (Note 4)	52/91		1799
			SS 35/38		
		Parish Church	85/94		pre-1800
			SS 72/74		
West Farndon	hamlet	Wesleyan	/ave110	ave 90	c.1828

Warwickshire Parishes

Parish	Population 1851	Denomination	am/pm	Evening	Date
Brailes	1,284	Wesleyan (Note 5(a))		25	
		Primitive Methodist	/70	80	1848
		(Note 5(b))	/SS 8	SS 8	
		Friends (Note 5(c))	ave 8		C17
		Catholic (Note 5(d))	130/80		1726
		Parish Ch. (Note 5(e))	160/206		pre-1800
			SS 72/72		
Kineton	1,023	Parish Church	c.300/c.400		pre-1800
			SS 87/87		
		Wesleyan	32	89	1842
			SS 37		
Little Kineton	hamlet	Independent/Baptist		55	c.1796
			SS 13	SS 13	
Middle Tysoe	1,049	Wesleyan	91	115	pre-1800
			SS 94		
		Primitive Methodist	70	70	1844
		Parish Church	150/200		pre-1800

Table 4 shows the number of Dissenting chapels and meeting houses in Banburyshire compared to the county of Oxfordshire on 30 March 1851.[2] The figures confirm the strong concentration of Dissent in the region, with 92 chapels and meeting-houses, compared to 240 in the whole of Oxfordshire. They also show that, on average, there were about two Dissenting chapels or meeting-houses per parish in Banburyshire compared to less than one in Oxfordshire.

The table shows that, of the total Dissenting chapels and meeting-houses in Banburyshire, the Methodists provided 61%, but only 49% in Oxfordshire.

| Table 4 | Number of Dissenting chapels and meeting-houses in Banburyshire compared to Oxfordshire, 30 March 1851 | | | |

	Banburyshire		Oxfordshire	
Denomination	Dissent	CofE	Dissent	CofE
Wesleyan Methodist	38		76	
Primitive Methodist	19		42	
Independent/Congregational	11		43	
Baptist	8		38	
Particular/Strict Baptist	5		14	
Quakers	5		12	
Roman Catholic	4		8	
Other (Moravian)	2		7	
	92	44	240	257

In contrast, the percentages for Independents or Congregationalists (11%) and Baptists (14%) were significantly lower than the 18% and 22% in Oxfordshire. This provides support for the theory that Methodism made its strongest impact in areas where there was little if any Old Dissent i.e. Baptists and Independents.

Banbury Nonconformists

The population of Banbury in 1851 was 8,793. The 1851 religious census for Banbury (Table 3a) shows that total attendance was 6,180. If we take a simple reading of the figures, attendance represented 70% of the population. Significantly, 46% (2,880) of the attendance was at the various Nonconformist and Catholic chapels. However, this does not take into account the number of people attending morning and afternoon services at St Mary's Parish Church and the possible number of Dissenters attending other services. If we assume that half of those attending the morning service at St Mary's i.e. 650, also attended afternoon service, this would reduce total attendance to 5,530 or 62% of the total population. This is a high percentage compared to the overall findings for England and Wales, which showed that only some 50% of the population attended a service, but Banbury seems to have been very active on the religious front, as shown in Table 5 below. Attendance by Dissenters and Roman Catholics (2,880) represents 52% of the revised figure for total attendance. This is very much in line with the overall findings but it is significantly higher than elsewhere in Oxfordshire.

Table 5	Places of worship in Banbury, 1839-1906 based on trade directories			
Chapel/Church	1839	1860	1880	1906
St Mary's & St Paul's, Anglican	*	*	*	*
Baptist Chapel, South Bar	*			
Bridge St		*	*	*
Calvinist, West Bar	*			
West St		*	*	*
Ebenezer Chapel, Dashwood Rd			*	*
English Presbyterian, Horse Fair	*			
Independent, Church Lane	*			
South St		*		
South Bar			*	
Congregational Church, S.Bar				*
Primitive Methodist, Broad St	*	*		
Church Lane			*	*
Roman Catholic, South Bar	*	*	*	*
Society of Friends, Horse Fair	*	*	*	*
Unitarian, Church Lane		*	*	*
Wesleyan, Church Lane	*	*		
Marlborough Road			*	*
West St, Grimsbury			*	*
Disciples of Christ, Gatteridge St			*	
Plymouth Brethren, Church Lane			*	
Cadbury Memorial Hall				*
Salvation Army,Fortress, Fish St				*

Table 5, which shows no fewer than 15 places of worship in Banbury in 1839-1906, lends further support to W.T. Henderson's comments about the variety of religious denominations available in Banbury. As it is only based on entries in Rusher's Lists and other trade directories, there may well have been more religious meetings which were not publicised.

Chapter 3

Methodists (New Dissent)

'METHODISM, AS PRACTISED THERE, was a poor people's religion, simple and crude; but its adherents brought to it more fervour than was shown by the church congregation, and appeared to obtain more comfort and support from it than the church could give. Their lives were exemplary'.[1]

This was Flora Thompson's conclusion on Methodism in Juniper Hill in the 1880s and why it was different from the Church of England. The same might have been said much earlier in the late eighteenth and early nineteenth centuries, when the Church of England was generally weak and had little to offer to the local congregations. It was in this period that John Wesley and the Methodists emerged on the scene to provide the significant comfort and support which the Church could not give. There were a number of splinter groups within Methodism but only three of them were of significance locally: the Wesleyan and Primitive Methodists and Wesleyan Reform, so I have limited my examination to them.

a) Wesleyan Methodists

John Wesley (1703-91) (Plate 1), and his brother, Charles (1707-88), led a small group for study, prayer and good works from 1729, while they were at Oxford. Their discipline and fastidious habits earned them nicknames including 'the Holy Club', 'Bible Moths' and lastingly, 'Methodists'. In 1728 three Moravian societies had come to London and Oxford. The Moravians were a revivalist Protestant sect, which claimed to trace its origins to Bohemia and Moravia in the fifteenth century. John and Charles both converted to the sect but soon parted company to form their own sect, the Methodists. It is interesting that until recently there were two Moravian churches locally, in Eydon (pictured) and Woodford Halse (Plate 3). On 24 May 1738 John Wesley had a life-changing experience at a religious society meeting in Aldersgate Street, London: 'About a quarter to nine, while (the reader) was describing the change which God works in the heart through faith in Christ, I felt my heart strangely warmed'. In May 1739 he laid the foundation stone

Moravian church, Eydon, built in 1818, replacing one built in 1799, c. 1920. It is now closed. © OCC

of his first 'preaching house', the New Room in Bristol. In the same year he started to use The Foundery in Moorfields (the old cannon foundry) as a chapel. In 1778 the Foundery was replaced with Wesley's Chapel on City Road, which today is the cathedral of Methodism. In 1784 the annual Conference, which had first met in 1744, was legalised by the *Deed of Declaration* with the agreement of the 'legal hundred' itinerant preachers, who ratified Conference decisions. It was also in 1784 that Wesley, aged 81, preached in Banbury, at the Presbyterian Meeting House off Horsefair. He had never seen 'a people who appeared more ready prepared for the Lord'. In contrast, he described Towcester as a 'poor dead' place, while 'the inhabitants of Brackley understood him no better than if he had been talking Greek'.

From the 1740s Wesley started riding all over England, setting up 'societies' and smaller groups. He is thought to have notched up some 225,000 miles on horseback, somehow reading and scribbling notes as he rode. He also quickly recruited a young group of itinerant preachers, under his strict control, and locally based people who became the 'local preachers' and established preaching houses. From the late 1750s, in spite of Wesley's reluctance, it became increasingly common for these preaching houses to be registered as Dissenting places of worship under the Toleration Act. Wesley himself was always very reluctant to be seen as a Dissenter from the Church of England. An excerpt from the Wesleyan Register of Yeadon, near Leeds, in 1806[2] gives some idea of the enormous impact which the 'enthusiasm' of Wesley and his new movement could have on a small community. In dramatic, and almost poetic, language the writer speaks of '340 souls being wrested out of the hands of the divel; and restored to their proper owner the Lord Jesus Christ in the short space of a few weeks':

> And now my very dear brethren, what remains, but just to refresh
> your memorys on that blessed subject of the late great revival of the
> work of God amongst us! I doubt not but it is written on all your hearts

in the Indelible Characters of gratitude and thankfulness to God, it is not long since since Mr Wesley remarked that "In no part of England is the Gospel propegated with so much facility or so deeply rooted in the hearts of those that hear it, as in Yorkshire." If then Yorkshire (in the above sence) be the best part of England, I cannot hesitate to say that Yeadon (by Grace) is the best part of Yorkshire.

Did ever any of us hear of such a thing, did we ever see such a thing, did we ever read of such a thing as 340 souls being wrested out of the hands of the divel; and restored to their proper owner the Lord Jesus Christ in the short space of a few weeks; especially if we consider the size of our viluge which does not contain 300 families, but when did this great event happen? O my friends the recording angel of God has Noted it in heaven, shall we not record it on earth, Yes, let it be registered with pointed steel on tables of marble, let it be written by the finger of God on all our hearts—Its beginning is dated 27 day of January 1806 and continued in a great degree for Three Months.

John Yeadon

This so-called 'enthusiasm' of Wesley and his preachers was one aspect of the Methodists which the eighteenth-century Church of England found difficult to accept. Although the Methodists are often referred to as New Dissent, they themselves were not sure whether they were Dissenters. John Wesley always stated that he had no wish to leave the Church of England, although he was highly critical of it and his actions made separation probable. He expected the members of these new societies to continue to support their parish church, by attending Morning Prayer and Holy Communion, while the main Methodist services were typically in the afternoon and evening. However, new feasts and fasts were also developed in Wesley's Connexion as he called it, including the *Preaching Service*, which combined sermon, extempore prayer and the singing of Charles Wesley's hymns. Singing was a vital part of John Wesley's religious life and it became so for all Methodists, particularly the Primitive Methodists. There was also *The Love Feast*, borrowed from the Moravians, which became a democratic folk meal with bread and water handed round using a common cup, with personal testimonies and hymns. We shall look at the membership in more detail below but it is worth mentioning at this stage that the appeal of Methodism was mainly to the working-class and the poor and there was never any suggestion that it would influence the upper classes.

After Wesley's death, 'Methodist history was littered with schism from the 1790s to the 1850s'.[3] There is no need to dwell on most of the splinter groups, since they played little part on the local scene. They included the Kilhamites (New Connexion) (1797), the Independent Methodists (1806), the Bible Christians (1815) and the Protestant Methodists (1828). The most important splinter group in the region has been the Primitive Methodists, who were formed in 1810-11, and 1812 saw the formal split between the Church of England and the Methodists. In 1836, the first meeting of the Wesleyan Association was held. The Wesleyan Methodists, after a peak of 4.47% nationally in 1841, lost some 100,000 members in the early 1850s, as a result of the 'Fly Sheet' disruptions of 1846-9 and the secession of the Wesleyan Reformers in 1849.[4] The first Fly Sheet was published by James Everett in 1844, complaining of tyranny, undue centralisation and misuse of Connexional money. This was aimed at Jabez Bunting (1779-1858), the dominant manager of the Methodists for many years and also president of Conference many times. He was also a great preacher but many were critical of his dominant position, with one irritated Mancunian declaring that 'the whole Methodist Conference is buttoned up in a single pair of breeches'.[5]

It was at this point that Methodism in Chadwick's memorable phrase 'began to suffer a touch of melancholy, shadow of that partial loss of assurance which affected contemporary Anglicans'.[6] In spite of these divisions, the number worshipping in Wesleyan chapels at the evening services on 30 March 1851 was some 654,000. Nationally, Methodist membership recovered with the religious revival of the late 1850s and by 1863 there were 4.25 Methodists per 100 people over 15. They retained much of this membership during the 1870s and 1880s but thereafter decline set in again.[7] In 1857, the Wesleyan Association united with most of the splinter groups to form the United Methodist Free Church. In 1859, the remaining minority formed the Wesleyan Reform Union. In 1932, the Methodist Church was formed with the coming together of United Methodist, Primitive Methodist and Wesleyan Methodist Churches but not the Wesleyan Reform Union. There may have been as many as 800,000 members of the Methodist churches in the early twentieth century. By 2010 membership of the British Methodist Church had declined to some 238,000, although it still has some 5,000 church communities and over 800,000 people in Britain who have an active connection with the Methodist Church.

The great ambition of the Methodists in particular has always been to build their own chapel. We shall see below just how successful they have been in Banburyshire, and how influential the chapel has always been in the lives of Methodists. Singing too has always played a vital role, not only because of

John Wesley's influence but also because many of the early converts were illiterate and the singing of memorable hymns was a perfect way to their hearts. This was particularly true of the Primitive Methodists, the 'simple folk' as they sometimes described themselves, who were originally called Ranters because of their habit of singing in the street. The Wesleys, Charles, his son, Samuel (1766-1837), and grandson, Samuel Sebastian (1710-76), wrote literally thousands of hymns, many of them sung to this day in Anglican churches and Methodist chapels alike. Charles's best known hymns include 'Love divine, all loves excelling' and 'O thou who camest from above' (tune by S.S.Wesley). Later, Isaac Watts (1674-1748), a Nonconformist minister, contributed many great hymns, including 'When I survey the wondrous Cross', 'O God, our help in ages past', and the beautiful 'Give us the wings of faith to rise'.

Tables 6(a) and 6(b) show the Wesleyan Methodist Meetings in Banburyshire, 1784-2012. Table 6(a) lists the twenty which are still open, while Table 6(b) lists the twenty-seven where the chapels and meeting-houses have been closed and the meetings are no longer active. All the villages in both tables are or have been members of the Banbury Methodist Circuit, except the Bartons, Hook Norton, Sibford Gower, South Newington, Swerford and Wigginton. These have all been members of the Chipping Norton Circuit and Sibford Gower and Wigginton are still members. See Table 7 below for more details on the membership of the Banbury Circuit. Although the Wesleyans were strongest in the Midland cities, the West Riding of Yorkshire and in the South West, these tables do show their strength in rural Banburyshire as well as in Banbury itself. Old Dissent, in the form of the Baptists and Independents, was comparatively weak in the region and this allowed the Methodists to make swift progress. As we have seen, the weakness of the Church of England in the late eighteenth and early nineteenth centuries was also a contributing factor.

Notes to Table 6(a)

Banbury

1. Banbury's population of 8,793 in 1851 included Grimsbury and Neithrop.

2. *Marlborough Road*

There may have been a Methodist Meeting in Banbury as early as 1784, when John Wesley came to preach, but their first chapel was opened in Calthorpe Street in 1791. In 1812 they built a chapel in Church Lane, which was enlarged in 1828. In 1865 it was sold to the Primitive Methodists, and they

Marlborough Road Methodist Church, Banbury, buit 1865. Photo taken in 1978 just before the Sunday School (in the foreground) was pulled down. © OCC

moved to the new Marlborough Road chapel (pictured), described 'as Cathedral like'. This went underwent major reconstruction in 1975 and the congregation is still very active.

3. *Grimsbury*

A Methodist society was founded here in 1812. In 1858 a tiny chapel and Sunday school were opened in North Street. In 1871 a handsome new chapel was opened in West Street and it was greatly enlarged in 1876. In 1889 Grimsbury became part of the borough of Banbury. In 1986 the old chapel was pulled down and replaced with a modern church, which is shared with the Baptists.

4. *Neithrop*

Meeting places were registered in 1810, 1815 and 1825. The Mission Hall was built in Boxhedge in 1887 and is still active.

5. *Easington*

The church was built on Grange Road in 1938 and numbers are growing.

6. *Fairway*

The church was built in 1957 after class meetings had been held in the area for some years. The church is likely to be demolished shortly, the site redeveloped, and a new church built.

7. *St Francis Local Ecumenical Partnership* (LEP)

The church was built on Highlands Road, off Ruscote Avenue, in 1992, on land bought by the Catholics for an ecumenical church. The trustees include

Table 6(a) Wesleyan Methodist Meetings in Banburyshire, 1784-2012 Open Chapels and Churches					
Parish	Population 1851	Premises	Services 30 March 1851 am/pm	Evening	Date of first Meeting
Banbury	8,793				Note 1
Marlborough Road		church	361/118 SS 197	470	1784 Note 2
Grimsbury		church			1858 Note 3
Neithrop		church			1873 Note 4
Easington		church			1930s Note 5
Fairway		church			c.1950 Note 6
St Francis		church			1970s Note 7
Villages					
Adderbury East	978	chapel	/23 SS 12/12	36	1810 Note 8
Boddingt'n (Upper)	399	chapel (N)			1865 Note 9
Bodicote	673	chapel	SS 54	60	1846 Note 10
Chacombe	506	chapel (N)	93	107	1816 Note 11
Cropredy	596	chapel	73 SS 45/56	90 SS 10	1819 Note 12
Greatworth	135	chapel (N)	/80	80	1844 Note 13
Hornton	591	chapel	/102	140	1842 Note 14
Kineton	1,023	chapel(W)	32 SS 37	89	1842 Note 15
Middleton Cheney	1,330	chapel (N)	194/SS 48	265	1810 Note 16
Sibford Gower	549	chapel	/100 /SS 30	90	1827 Note 17
Tysoe (Middle)	1,049	chapel(W)	91 SS 94	115	1770 Note 18
Wigginton Woodford	314	chapel			1834 Note 19
Halse	800	chapel (N)			1808 Note 20
Wroxton	789	chapel	78	43	c.1820 Note 21
N = Northamptonshire, W = Warwickshire					

Methodists, United Reform Church, Catholics and Anglicans. Originally, they also included the Southam Brethren. There are close links with Marlborough Road Methodists, St Mary's Anglican, and St John's Roman Catholic, but not with the Baptists.

Wesleyan Methodist Church, Adderbury East, built in 1893. Photographed in the 1920s.
© OCC

Villages

8. *Adderbury East*

In 1810 a chapel (pictured) was built at the end of Chapel Lane; it was sold in 1927. In 1893 the new chapel was built to seat 200 and it remains active. The foundation stones include the names of William Mewburn and the Morris brothers.

9. *Upper Boddington*

Methodism infiltrated from Tysoe to both the Boddingtons by 1797-8, when two houses were registered. A chapel was not built until 1865 and most of the local Methodists went to Lower Boddington after a chapel was built there in 1836. The new chapel opened on Frog Lane in 1865. It was extended in 1885 and it is still active.

10. *Bodicote*

In 1802 the vicar reported the existence of a lively group of Methodists, probably using a licensed meeting-house. A datestone on the chapel in East Street says 'Erected in 1845'. It was a member of the Deddington Wesleyan Reform Circuit for a period but later joined the Banbury Methodist Circuit. It is still active.

11. *Chacombe*

A chapel was erected in 1816. A new one was opened in 1873 and it is still active.

Wesleyan Methodist Chapel, Cropredy, built in 1881, photographed in the 1920s.
© OCC

12. *Cropredy*

A house was licensed in 1819 and in 1821 a stable was converted into a chapel, which later became the Post Office. In 1866 one fifth of the village were said to be Dissenters. In 1881 a new larger chapel and Sunday school were built by Thomas Cherry (pictured) for £700 and it is still active.

13. *Greatworth*

The Methodists were meeting by 1832. The first chapel was erected in 1844 and a new one was built on the same site in 1860 (Plate 4). In 1861 they were transferred from the Brackley to the Banbury Circuit. In 1878 a schoolroom was built next to the chapel. The chapel is still active.

14. *Hornton*

The chapel was Primitive Methodist until 1947, when the Banbury Primitive Methodist Circuit was closed and the remaining members joined the Wesleyans. It is still an active member of the Banbury Methodist Circuit and it is also in an Ecumenical Partnership (LEP) with Horley Anglicans. Horley Methodist chapel is now a private dwelling.

15. *Kineton*

The Methodists were meeting by 1832 but did not build a chapel until 1842.

In 1846 the Kineton Circuit with 13 members was separated from the Banbury Circuit. The foundation stone for a new chapel on the same site was laid on 21 June 1893. A Schoolroom extension was added in 1954. The chapel is still an active member of the Mid-Warwickshire Methodist Circuit.

16. *Middleton Cheney*

In 1814 a new building was registered as the Methodist chapel. A new chapel was built in 1867 to seat 400, and a church hall next door in 1907. It is still active.

17. *Sibford Gower*

The Wesleyans were meeting in a house by 1823. A chapel was built in Temple Mill Road by 1827 and rebuilt in 1864. It is still active.

18. *Middle Tysoe*

Methodism had been established in the Tysoe area by about 1770 and they were early members of the Banbury Circuit when it was formed in 1793. By 1804 they had joined the informal Kineton Circuit. They met in a house until 1821, when they bought two cottages and a barn, which they converted into a chapel, where they were to worship for the next 149 years. A gallery was added and the chapel was renovated about 1868, with the addition of new pews. A Sunday School was also added sometime after this. The chapel was finally pulled down in 1970 and a new chapel was built on Main Street. It is still an active member of the Mid-Warwickshire Methodist Circuit.

19. *Wigginton*

A house was registered in 1834 and in 1877 the Wesleyans may have been meeting in The Old House in Chapel Lane. The chapel was built in 1877 and it is still an active member of the Chipping Norton Circuit.

20. *Woodford Halse (Hinton)*

There was early Methodism in Hinton and buildings were registered in 1808 and 1813. Hinton Malt House was registered as a chapel when the Methodists moved from West Farndon. A new chapel was erected in 1879 (now a private dwelling) but it was replaced by a larger one next door in 1902 (Plate 5). The old chapel became the schoolroom at this point. The Great Central Railway Extension had led to a growth in population and need for this larger chapel. Hinton was a member of the Brackley Circuit from 1886 to 1893, when it transferred to the Banbury Circuit, of which it is still an active member.

21. *Wroxton*

The first mention of a Methodist community is in 1778. In 1822 William Gardner's house was registered as a meeting place, and a chapel may have been built then. In 1864 the chapel was rebuilt and was still in use in 1965. It is now the garage of Sundial Farmhouse on the Green. In 1935 the Goodman

Chapel was built on High Street in memory of the Revd John Goodman. Support has declined and the chapel is likely to close shortly.

Notes to Table 6(b)

1. *Balscott*

A hamlet in Wroxton parish. A meeting-house was licensed in 1805 and in 1808 there were '10 Calvinistic Methodists' here. A chapel was not built until 1850. It closed recently and is now a private dwelling.

2. *Middle Barton*

A hamlet and township in Steeple Barton parish. A chapel was built in Worton Road (formerly Chapel Street) in 1835. It was closed by 1939 and sold in 1952. There may have been an earlier chapel in Westcott Barton in 1814.

3. *Bloxham*

A house was registered in 1821 and a chapel had been built by 1853. In 1868 a new chapel was built in Chapel Street. By 1965 it seated 250. It was later sold to Bloxham School and is now the Wesley Theatre.

4. *Lower Boddington*

Methodism infiltrated from Tysoe to both the Boddingtons by 1797-8, when two houses were registered. In 1836 a building was registered as a chapel. A new chapel was built in 1888. It closed in 1967 and is now a private dwelling.

5. *Great Bourton*

In 1790 a licence was obtained for a building owned by William Claridge, a butcher. A chapel was built on his land in 1792. In 1814 the vicar reported that about half the inhabitants were Dissenters, with Antipaedo Baptists, Presbyterians and Methodists all attending the same chapel. There were later moves towards Unitarianism and Congregationalism. By 1866, it was 'Independent in the morning and anything in the evening'. In 1924 the remaining Congregational trustees sold the dilapidated chapel to the Wesleyans, who built a new red brick chapel in 1932. It closed about 2000 and is now the village hall.

6. *Brailes*

The Weslyans met in a house initially and later used the Quakers' meeting-house. Later still they built a chapel in the centre of the village. This was sold some time after the Union in 1932, and they moved to the Primitive Methodist chapel. That too is now closed.

7. *Byfield*

A chapel hut was erected in 1937. It was closed in 1972 and moved to the Ford Sports Ground in Daventry as a pavilion. The ground is now closed and the hut was presumably scrapped.

Table 6(b) Wesleyan Methodist Meetings in Banburyshire, 1784-2012
Closed Chapels and Meeting-houses

Parish	Population 1851	Premises	Services 30 March 1851 am/pm	Evening	Date of first meeting
Balscott	hamlet	chapel	51	95	1805 Note 1
Barton (Middle)	hamlet	chapel	181 SS /4045	188	1814 Note 2
Bloxham	1,336	house	/126 /SS 27	120	1821 Note 3
Boddingt'n (Lower)	327	chapel (N)	/50	57	1836 Note 4
Bourton (Great)	573	chapel			1923 Note 5
Brailes	1,284	house (W)		25	pre-1800 Note 6
Byfield	1,021	chapel (N)			1937 Note 7
Caulcott	hamlet	chapel	/80	88	1830 Note 8
Chipping Warden	521	chapel (N)	/86 /SS 23	81 SS 13	c.1807 Note 9
Clifton	hamlet	chapel	50/40		c.1815 Note 10
Cottisford	263	cottage		30	1844 Note 11
Eydon	621	chapel (N)			1860 Note 12
Hanwell	301	house		47	1822 Note 13
Hethe	418	chapel	30/60	50	1794 Note 14
Heyford (Lower)	605	chapel	ave 50		1804 Note 15
Heyford (Upper)	399	chapel	22/92	101	1829 Note 16
Hook Norton	1,496	chapel	/100 /SS 74	160	1794 Note 17
Horley	392	chapel	75	90	1794 Note 18
King's Sutton	1,335	chapel (N)	15/53		1820 Note 19
North Newington	436	houses			1805-20 Note 20
Shottesw'll	328	house (W)			1834 Note 21
Shutford	416	chapel	95	112	1808 Note 22
South Newington	419	chapel		110	1822 Note 23
Sulgrave	604	chapel (N)			1863 Note 24
Wardingt'n	861	chapel	/126	127	1815 Note 25
Warmingt'r	523	chapel (W)			1790s Note 26
West Farndon	hamlet	chapel	/ave 110	ave 90	c.1828 Note 27

N = Northamptonshire, W = Warwickshire

8. *Caulcott*

A hamlet in Lower Heyford parish. A house was registered in 1830 and a chapel was built in 1841. It was in use until 1955 when it became a garage.

9. *Chipping Warden*

A chapel was built about 1807, re-erected in 1844 and rebuilt in 1884. It closed recently and has been sold.

10. *Clifton*

A hamlet/township in Deddington parish. The 1815 'chapel' may have been the cottage called the Tabernacle in Pepper Alley, which was demolished in the 1950s. A new chapel was opened in 1869 and it was still in use in the 1950s. It was sold about 1974 and is now a private dwelling.

11. *Cottisford*

Methodists, described as Wesleyans in 1851, met in Thomas Lavine's cottage in Juniper Hill. In the 1880s, in Flora Thompson's time, they were described as Ranters and were viewed with some suspicion by the inspectors. However, they were members of the Brackley Wesleyan Methodist Circuit from 1878 to at least 1896, when there was only one service a month. They probably ceased to meet soon afterwards.

12. *Eydon*

Methodism began here in 1812, and a barn was registered in 1820. The present building at 55 High Street was erected in 1860 (pictured). It is now closed but has not yet been redeveloped.

Wesleyan Methodist Chapel, Eydon, built in 1860, now closed. Drawn by Robin Stagg, 2012. © Robin Stagg.

13. *Hanwell*

William Gunn's house was licensed in 1822 and a chapel was built late in the nineteenth century. A new chapel was opened in 1921 but it closed in 1966.

14. *Hethe*

Various houses were licensed from 1794. By 1854 a chapel had been built. A new one was built in 1876. It closed in the late 1960s and is now a private dwelling.

15. *Lower Heyford*

A house was registered in 1804 and a chapel built soon after, next to Forge House. A new chapel was built in Mill Lane in 1904. In the 1940s and 1950s it was used as a Baptist Chapel by the US Forces from the Upper Heyford Base. It was then closed.

16. *Upper Heyford*

From 1826 a room in William Austin's house was used, until a chapel was built in 1829. A new chapel was opened in 1867 and closed in 1966. In 1849 another meeting-house was licensed, probably for the Reformers. It was only in use until the 1880s.

17. *Hook Norton*

Methodists first met in a house in 1794. They may have built a chapel on Down Street in 1813. By 1829 they owned land on Wells Close, near Tite Lane, where they built a chapel later. In 1875 they built an impressive new chapel on Chapel Street, off Mobbs Lane. The chapel was wrecked by a gale in 1985 and sold in 1986.

18. *Horley*

In 1794 this was the first Methodist chapel to be built outside Banbury. It was enlarged about 1840. It was still active in 1969 but it is now a private house.

19. *King's Sutton*

From 1820 Methodists met in various houses, until they built a thatched stone chapel next to Home Farm in 1856. Their name was changed then to The Primitive Methodist Connexion. A new chapel was built in 1936, on the corner of Newlands. It closed about 1995.

20. *North Newington*

There were meetings in various houses from 1805-1820, and there are references to a chapel next to Wash House, which must have closed many years ago.

21. *Shotteswell*

In 1798 James Hawtin's house was registered and in 1805 a chapel was registered. A new chapel was built in 1854 but I have been unable to trace any entry in the 1851 religious census. The chapel closed in 1971 and it is now a private dwelling.

22. *Shutford*

Methodists were first recorded here in 1808. Two 'chapels' were licensed in 1826 and 1827. A new chapel was built in 1857; it closed in 1972.

23. *South Newington*

William Taylor's house was registered in 1822. By 1847 they were leasing the 1692 Friends' meeting-house. From 1857 the congregation was said to be Primitive Methodist and they built a chapel in 1875.

24. *Sulgrave*

There may have been a number of houses registered for the Methodists between 1826 and 1834 but a chapel on Manor Road was not erected until 1863. It is now a private house.

25. *Wardington*

Houses were registered in 1815/16 and a chapel was built in 1827. In 1895 it was sold to George Loveday and a new chapel (datestone 1896) was built on an adjoining site. It was still active in 1964 but it was sold in 1971. It is now a private dwelling.

26 *Warmington*

A house was registered in 1794. A chapel was built in 1811 but I have been unable to trace any entry in the 1851 religious census. This was the oldest active chapel on the Banbury Circuit, until it closed in 2009. It will be sold when planning permission is given.

27. *West Farndon*

A hamlet of Woodford Halse. Farndon Mill was registered for worship in 1920. A chapel was built about 1828 and joined the Banbury Circuit in 1829. It closed in 1861 and in 1862 the Methodists moved to Hinton where the Malt House was opened as a chapel.

Banbury Methodist Circuit

The Banbury Methodist Society was at first part of the Northampton Circuit. They built their first chapel in 1791 on Calthorpe Street and from 1793-1796 it became the centre of a new Banbury Circuit formed from the western part of the Northampton Circuit. It included Brackley, Buckingham and Tysoe, with a total of 210 members in 12 towns and villages. The years 1797-1803 saw Banbury lose its position as circuit chapel to Brackley but it regained its position in 1804.

Table 7, which is compiled from Wesleyan Preacher Plans, shows the Members of the Banbury Methodist Circuit, 1814-2012. It shows how far the circuit initially crossed county boundaries into Northamptonshire and Warwickshire and in 1846 it was divided into the Banbury and Kineton

Table 7 Members of the Banbury Methodist Circuit, 1814-2012 (Note)					
Members	1814	1828	1848	1933	2012
Banbury	*	*	*	*	*
Adderbury	*	*	*	*	*
Boddington(Lower)(N)	*	*	*	*	
Combrook (W)	*	*	K		
Eatington (W)	*	*	K		
Drayton	*	*			
N.Newington	*	*			
Harbury (W)	*	*			
Horley	*	*	*	*	*
Knightcote (W)	*	*	K		
Northend (W)	*	*	K		
Middleton Cheney (N)	*	*	*	*	*
Oxhill (W)	*	*	K		
Tysoe (W)	*	*	K		
Shutford	*	*	*	*	
Tadmarton	*	*			
Shotswell (W)	*	*	*	*	
Balscot		*	*	*	
Bloxham		*	*	*	
Bodicote		*	*	*	*
(Butlers) Marston (W)		*	K		
Chacombe (N)		*	*	*	*
Chipping Warden (N)		*	*	*	
Cropredy		*	*	*	*
Fenny Compton (W)		*	K		
Hanwell		*	*	*	
King's Sutton (N)		*	*		
Mollington (W)		*			
Nethercote		*			
Pillerton Priors (W)		*	K		
Ratley (W)		*	K		
Wardington		*	*	*	
Warmington (W)		*	*	*	
Wroxton		*	*	*	*
Bourton (Little)			*	*	
(West) Farndon (N)			*		
Whatcote (W)			K		
South Newington			*		
Eydon (N)				*	
Greatworth (N)				*	*
Grimsbury				*	*
Hinton (N)				*	*

Table 7 continued	Members of the Banbury Methodist Circuit, 1814-2012 (Note)			
Members	1814	1828	1848	1933
Sulgrave (N)				*
Boddington (Upper) (N)				*
Neithrop				*
Bourton (Great)				*
Byfield (N)				*
Fairway, Banbury				
Easington, Banbury				
St Francis, Banbury				
	17	34	21	27

K = a member of the Kineton Wesleyan Methodist Circuit, formed in 1846. The chapels were in Oxfordshire (23), except for those marked N for Northamptonshire (12) or W for Warwickshire (15).

Circuits. The former included 21 village chapels and the latter 13. The Kineton Circuit is now a section of the Mid-Warwickshire Methodist Circuit with five members; Leamington is the other section with eight members. In 1932, the Methodist Church was formed with the coming together of United Methodist, Primitive Methodist and Wesleyan Methodist Churches. However, it was not until 1947 that the Banbury Primitive Methodist circuit ceased to operate as a separate entity. Amalgamation took place then under the leadership of the Marlborough Road Church in Banbury.

The table shows the continuing strength of the Wesleyans in the region up to 1933. In 1947 they received a boost on the amalgamation with the local Primitive Methodist circuit, although there were only eleven active Primitive Methodist chapels by then. There has also been some expansion in Banbury subsequently and the following sixteen chapels are now members of the circuit. In Banbury: Marlborough Road, Easington, Fairway, Grimsbury, Neithrop and St Francis LEP. In the villages: Adderbury, Bodicote, Chacombe, Cropredy, Greatworth, Hinton (Woodford Halse), Hornton-with-Horley, Middleton Cheney, Upper Boddington and Wroxton.

Sadly a number of rural chapels have closed recently and Wroxton seems likely to close shortly.

b) Primitive Methodists

The Primitive Methodists were by far the largest and most important of the splinter groups of Methodism. One Sunday in May 1807, wheelwright Hugh Bourne climbed to the top of Mow Cop, a rocky hill high on the borders of Cheshire and Staffordshire, to launch the Primitive Methodist movement, holding a 12-hour meeting with friends interested in returning to a simpler form of worship. Initially the group were called The 'Camp Meeting Methodists' but they were organised into a separate movement in 1810-11, after Hugh Bourne and William Clowes were expelled from Wesleyan Methodism for holding camp meetings. These meetings were seen as 'highly improper and likely to be of considerable mischief'.[8] In 1812 the name Primitive Methodists was adopted, although they were also called 'Ranters' because of their habit of singing in the street. Margaret Gibbs, who comes from a long line of Tysoe 'Prims', as they were often called, has been organist for a number of chapels. When I asked her about the local union with the Wesleyans in 1936, she said, 'We may have brought them some problems but we brought them singing'. The 'Ranters' originated in Belper, near Derby, where one of their services included a remarkable contribution from 'this rugged Elijah of the coalpit, a hewer of coals for six days down in the deep dark mine, and a very flame of fire on the seventh'.[9] This gives some idea of their enthusiasm, which, like the Ranter name, tended to reinforce their image as a crude and unsophisticated movement, both in its character and in its members. However, by the time of the 1851 religious census, they were five times as large as any other seceded Methodist group, with nearly 230,000 worshipping in their chapels. This was roughly a third of the Wesleyan worshippers.

In the first half of the nineteenth century the Primitive Methodists were particularly successful in touching the poor or very poor, and they were clearly seen as the working-man's church. They also tended to favour lay people, including women, and they allowed women to preach. However, 'As the decades passed the social atmosphere of the Primitive chapel began to resemble that of the Wesleyan chapel; and yet till the end of the century they were nearer the poor, and were always more rural, whereas the Wesleyans remained more largely urban'.[10] They also played a significant role in establishing a union of farm workers in the 1870s and 1880s. The Wesleyans may have been more successful in the towns but in Banburyshire, as we have seen, they have also been strong in the rural communities, building nearly three times as many chapels as the Primitive Methodists (see Table 15).

Table 8 shows the Primitive Methodist Meetings in Banburyshire, 1811-1947, when the Banbury Primitive Methodist Circuit amalgamated with the Wesleyans, under the leadership of the Marlborough Road Church in Banbury. Some of these Meetings, like the Wesleyan ones, were members of the Chipping Norton Circuit. Only the Hornton chapel remains open, as a member of the Banbury Methodist Circuit.

Notes to Table 8

1. *Banbury*

In 1839 the Banbury Primitive Methodists opened a small meeting-house at the rear of two cottages in Broad Street. A chapel was built soon after and enlarged in 1847. In 1865 the congregation moved to Church Lane, having bought the chapel from the Wesleyans. This chapel was renovated in the 1920s and continued in use until 1947. The Broad Street chapel became a shop after 1865 and was demolished in 1933. Meetings were also held briefly in Neithrop, from 1873 to 1881.

2. *Middle Barton*

A chapel was built in 1860 in The Dock (pictured) and they became members of the Chipping Norton Circuit. The chapel was modernised in 1984 and continued in use until its closure very recently.

3. *Steeple Barton*

A chapel (now Chapel House) was built in Fox Lane in 1851 but closed in 1860 when the new chapel was built in The Dock (pictured). Fox Lane was still being used for lectures in 1875.

4. *Westcott Barton*

Ranters were recorded here in 1834. In 1851, their chapel may have been in the drive to Manor Farm.

5. *Little Bourton*

The Primitive Methodists were active in Great Bourton in 1835. However, their chapel was built in Little Bourton in 1845, on the corner of Chapel Lane

Primitive Methodist Chapel, The Dock, Middle Barton, built 1860, photograph c.1920. It closed recently. © OCC

Parish	Population 1851	Premises	Services 30 March 1851 am/pm	Evening	Date of first meeting

Table 8   Primitive Methodist Meetings in Banburyshire 1811-1947

Parish	Population 1851	Premises	Services 30 March 1851 am/pm	Evening	Date of first meeting
Banbury	8,793	chapel	72/123 SS 87/89	144	1839 Note 1
Villages					
Bartons					
(Middle)	hamlet	chapel			1860 Note 2
(Steeple)	757	chapel			1851 Note 3
(Westcott)	759	chapel	130	136	1834 Note 4
Bourton		chapel		45	1835 Note 5
(Little)	hamlet				
Brailes	1,284	chapel (W)	/70 /SS 8	80 SS 8	1848 Note 6
Byfield	1,021	chapel (N)	/50	100	1836 Note 7
Chacombe	506	chapel (N)	ave 50		c.1830 Note 8
Claydon	330	chapel	/46 /SS 5	50 SS 3	1835 Note 9
Deddingt'n	2,178	chapel			1858 Note 10
Duns Tew	452	cottage	53	65	1811 Note 11
Epwell	330	chapel	129 SS 16	150	1825 Note 12
F'thinghoe	416	chapel (N)	20	90	1860 Note 13
Heyford (Upper)	399	cottage	ave 40		1850s Note 14
Hook Norton	1,496	various	60	100	1846 Note 15
Horley	392	cottage		40	1831 Note 16
Hornton	591	chapel	102 SS 20/20	140	1836 Note 17
King's Sutton	1,335	chapel (N)			1856 Note 18
Ledwell	526	chapel			1856 Note 19
Middleton Cheney	1,330	cottage(N)	/100 /SS 63	110	1835 Note 20
Milton	164	chapel	/35 /SS 25	27	1830s Note 21
Mollington	241	chapel	60 SS16/16	86	1835 Note 22
Sheningt'n	437	chapel	80		c.1817 Note 23
Shutford	416	chapel			1857 Note 24

N = Northamptonshire, W = Warwickshire

Parish	Population 1851	Premises	Services 30 March 1851		Date of first meeting
			pm	Evening	
Sibford					
Gower	549	chapel			1869 Note 25
South					
Newington	419	chapel			1857 Note 26
Swerford	440	chapel			1864 Note 27
Tadmarton	450	chapel			c.1860 Note 28
Tysoe (Middle)	1,049	chapel	70	70	1844 Note 29
Warmingt'r Woodford	523	chapel (W)			1858 Note 30
Halse	800	chapel (N)			c.1840 Note 31

Table 8 continued — Primitive Methodist Meetings in Banburyshire 1811-1947

N = Northamptonshire, W = Warwickshire

and Uplands Rise (Plate 7). It was closed and sold in the 1980s, and is now a private dwelling.

6. *Brailes*

A chapel was registered in 1848 but the present substantial building, on the edge of Upper Brailes, was erected in 1863 (pictured). At the rear of the chapel is the old Sunday School building. The chapel was shared with the Wesleyans for many years but it closed recently and will be sold when planning permission is given.

7. *Byfield*

A chapel was built on Bell Lane in 1836. Initially there were 24 members, who joined the Banbury Circuit but they had ceased to be members by 1870. The chapel closed many years ago and only the railings remain.

8. *Chacombe*

A society was formed about 1830. There is some evidence that a chapel was built, as the vicar reported that it was disused in 1875. They were still members of the Banbury Circuit in 1894 but not in 1904.

9. *Claydon*

A meeting was active by 1835. The chapel was opened in 1846 and enlarged in 1861 (see plaque). It was last used in 1972 and is now the garage of a private house.

10. *Deddington*

A meeting may have been active by 1858 when the new Banbury Circuit was formed. A chapel was built in 1879, probably on New Street where the

Primitive Methodist Chapel, Brailes, interior, built 1863. Photo 1920s. It closed recently. © OCC

Salvation Army Barracks was established in 1898. It was said to have been formerly a 'little Bethel' i.e. a Primitive Methodist chapel. Deddington were still a member of the Banbury Circuit in 1904 but the meeting must have closed shortly after this.

11. *Duns Tew*

From 1811 various houses were registered as meeting places. In 1851 it was home to five Primitive Methodist preachers but a chapel was never built.

12. *Epwell*

A chapel was built about 1754 as a tithe barn but was used for worship by a Baptist society, which was registered in 1829. In 1825 the Primitive Methodist minister of Wellesbourne certified a revivalist chapel, the property of Thomas Marsh. In 1854 the old chapel was purchased for the Primitive Methodists. Their membership had risen to twenty by 1894 but had declined to ten by 1904. The chapel was closed in 1972 when membership had fallen to two.

13. *Farthinghoe*

The original chapel was built pre-1800, which pre-dates Primitive Methodism. A new chapel was built in 1860. In 1894 a new building was given to them, although it had been in use as a chapel since at least 1889. It closed in the early 1990s and is now a private dwelling.

14. *Upper Heyford*

A meeting-house, in use in the 1850s and 1860s, was described by the rector as a 'nuisance and disturbance' to the parish, and it closed soon after.

15. *Hook Norton*

The first meeting in 1846 was held in a barn. From 1881 to 1898 they leased the Quaker meeting-house in Southrop. There is mention of a chapel in a 1911 trade directory but other indications are that they met in the Old School Room and other venues. The congregation survived until the Union in 1932.

16. *Horley*

The house of William Salmons was licensed in 1831 but there is no mention of a chapel being built.

17. *Hornton*

A building was registered in 1836 and a chapel was built in 1842. A new one was built in 1884 (pictured). The old chapel became the Sunday School until it was sold in 1979. Hornton is still an active member of the Banbury Methodist Circuit, which they joined in 1947.

18. *King's Sutton*

The Methodists here changed their name to The Primitive Methodist Connexion when they built a new chapel on Richmond Street in 1856. It closed in 1936, when a new Methodist church was built up the road on Newlands. This closed in the early 1990s and is now a private dwelling.

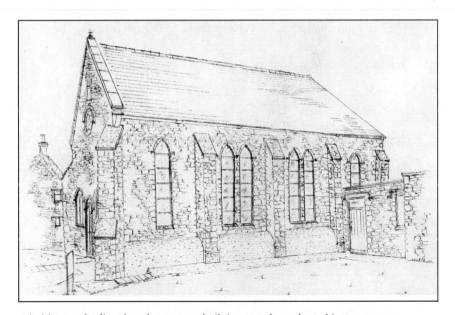

Primitive Methodist Chapel, Hornton, built in 1884, drawn by Robin Stagg, 2012.
© Robin Stagg

19. *Ledwell*

The chapel was opened in 1856 (see datestone) (Plate 9). Attendance was very high in the 1860s and 1870s, including many people from Sandford St Martin. It closed in 1954 and was sold in 1960.

20. *Middleton Cheney*

There was an active meeting by 1835 and they were still members of the Banbury Circuit in 1904 but no chapel was ever built.

21. *Milton*

The chapel is said to be pre-1800 and was probably built for the Presbyterians in the early eighteenth century. They ceased to use it by about 1842 and passed it on to the Primitive Methodists. Their tenure seems to have been brief as the Barford Anglicans were using it briefly in the 1850s.

22. *Mollington*

There were some houses registered by the Wesleyans 1817-28 but there was an active meeting of the Primitive Methodists by 1835. The impressive chapel was built by them in 1845 (Plate 8) but there were only ten members by 1896. It closed in 1947. It was acquired by the Plymouth Brethren in 1950 but was closed again in 1969. It is now a private house.

23. *Shenington*

The first meeting was about 1817 when they shared a room with the Independents. They built a chapel for themselves between 1852 and 1869. In 1878 the rector described them as 'very consequential and self-opinionated'. By 1884 Shenington had combined with Alkerton. The chapel closed in 1947.

24. *Shutford*

A chapel was recorded in 1869 and they were still members of the circuit in 1904.

25. *Sibford Gower*

They had a small chapel from 1869 until 1920, when they amalgamated with the Wesleyans.

26. *South Newington*

The Wesleyans leased the Friends' meeting-house from 1847. The 'Prims' took it on from 1857 until they built a chapel in 1875 (pictured). It closed in 1939. It is now a private dwelling but there is a datestone showing 'Primitive Methodest [sic] Chapel erected 1875', and the foundation stones survive with the names of the original subscribers.

27. *Swerford*

There was a meeting by 1864 in a timber/tin hut acquired from the rail-workers. Until recently it was still lying in a field between Wigginton and Milcombe. A chapel was built in 1879. In 1938 a new one was built on the site

Primitive Methodist Chapel, South Newington, built in 1875, photographed c.1920. It closed in 1939. © OCC

of the Old Forge and Post Office, which had burned down. It was sold in 1992 and is now a private dwelling.

28. *Tadmarton*

A chapel had been built by 1863 and it is marked on the first edition of the Ordinance Survey map of 1881. They were still members of the circuit in 1904.

29. *Middle Tysoe*

A chapel was built on Back Lane in 1844. They left it in 1936, when the 'Prims' and the Wesleyans amalgamated to form the Tysoe Methodist Society. The old chapel was taken over by the Plymouth Brethren but later the site became a coal yard.

30. *Warmington*

They met in what is now Thimble Cottage (red brick) from 1858 to c.1904. The dates on the plaque (1811-1960) are wrong but the chapel was demolished in 1960.

31. *Woodford Halse (Hinton)*

There was a Primitive Methodist Chapel in Hinton in 1842 but five years later it had disappeared.

Table 9   Members of the Banbury Primitive Methodist Circuit
1870-1947 (Note 1)

Members	1870	1884	1904	1932	1947
Banbury	*	*	*	*	*
Alkerton (Note 2)	*	*			
Brailes (W)	*	*	*	*	*
Butlers Marston (W)	*	*	*	*	*
Claydon	*	*	*	*	*
Chacombe (N)	*	*			
Deddington	*	*	*		
Epwell	*	*	*	*	*
Farnborough (W)	*				
Farthinghoe (N)	*	*	*	*	*
Hanwell	*	*			
Hornton (Note 3)	*	*	*	*	*
King's Sutton (N)	*	*	*	*	*
Middleton Cheney (N)	*	*	*		
Mollington	*	*	*	*	*
Radway (W)	*	*	*		
Ratley (W)	*	*			
Shenington (Note 2)	*	*	*	*	*
Shotteswell (W)	*				
Shutford	*	*	*		
Tadmarton	*	*	*		
Tysoe (Middle) (W)	*	*	*	*	*
Warmington (W)	*	*	*		
Winderton (W)	*				
	24	21	17	11	11

Notes to Table 9

1. The chapels were in Oxfordshire (11), except for those marked N for Northamptonshire (4) or W for Warwickshire (9).

2. By 1884 Alkerton and Shenington were combined.

3. Hornton and Tysoe are the only meetings still active, the former as a member of the Banbury Methodist Circuit, the latter of the Mid-Warwickshire Methodist Circuit.

Banbury Primitive Methodist Circuit

The Banbury Primitive Methodists were initially part of the Welton Circuit (near Daventry) sometime after 1836. In 1842 the Banbury Primitive Methodist Circuit was formed with about 250 members. A new circuit was formed in 1858 with 16 chapels, based at Church Lane Chapel, Banbury. By way of comparison, the Oxford Circuit was formed in 1845 and the Bicester one in 1846. Table 9 lists the members of the circuit between 1870 and 1947. The number was fairly stable, with a maximum of 24, although there were only 11 by 1932, the official date of the merger with the Wesleyans. However, it was not until 1947 that the Primitive Methodist circuit ceased to operate as a separate entity and amalgamation took place under the leadership of the Marlborough Road Church in Banbury.

The Wesleyans have clearly been stronger than the Primitive Methodists in the region, and the Primitive Methodists were generally strong where the Wesleyans were not. Locally, there have been only a few villages where the two groups have worshipped alongside each other: the Bartons, Brailes, Chacombe, Hook Norton, Horley, Middleton Cheney and Tysoe. In the Bartons, Brailes and Tysoe both groups built chapels, while in the other villages the Primitive Methodists failed to build one. We shall look more closely at the relationship between the two groups in Chapter 8. It remains to examine one other splinter group, Wesleyan Reform, since they too formed a circuit in the region.

c) Wesleyan Reform Union

As we have seen, the Fly Sheet disruptions (1846-9) led to expulsions and secessions of the Reformers from Wesleyan Methodism. They all objected to what they saw as excessive control from the centre. The majority of them united with the Wesleyan Association in 1857 to form the United Methodist Free Churches. A minority remained and sometime after 1859 they formed the Wesleyan Reform Union (WRU). The main point of difference for them with the Wesleyan Methodists was their desire for each church to have the right of administering its own affairs. Table 10 lists the Wesleyan Methodist Reform Meetings in Banburyshire, c.1860-2012. The table includes attendance figures for 30 March 1851, where applicable, to show the level of local support for the Methodists before the WRU was created. Where chapels were built, the first ones were all built before the WRU was formed; some replacement chapels were built later. Currently, the WRU has eleven circuits in England, with about one hundred chapels and some 1,400 members. Apart from circuits in High Wycombe and Wellingborough, most of them are in the North of England and the headquarters is in Sheffield.

Table 10   Wesleyan Reform Meetings in Banburyshire, c.1860-2012
(Notes 1-2)

Parish	Population 1851	Premises	Services 30 March 1851		Date of first chapel
			am/pm	Evening	
Open					
Deddington (Note 3)	2,178	chapel	/160	147	1800
Fritwell (Note 4)	514	chapel	/68	84	1847
Souldern (Note 5)	619	chapel	SS 50	108	1850
Syresham (Note 6)	1,027	chapel (N)	/166	183	1846
Closed					
Aynho (Note 7)	611	house (N)			n/a
Barford (Note 8)	392	chapel	40	92	1840
St Michael			SS 20	SS 30	
Bodicote (Note 9)	673	chapel	SS 54	60	1845
Croughton (Note10)	582	chapel (N)	25/60	120	1829
North Aston (Note 11)	308	house			n/a
SteepleAston(Note12)	601	chapel			1852
Stoke Lyne (Note 13)	631	house	68		n/a
Whitfield (Note 14)	326	chapel (N)			c.1823

Notes to Table 10

Open Chapels

1. A Deddington Wesleyan Reform Circuit was formed sometime after 1859 and the above meetings all appear on the 1879 Plan for the Circuit. Aynho and North Aston Methodists do not appear in the 1851 religious census and they never built chapels.

2. The surviving Wesleyan Reform chapels are no longer on a formal Deddington Circuit, since Deddington withdrew some twenty years ago. However, Fritwell, Souldern and Syresham still operate an informal circuit.

3. *Deddington*

In 1798 Charles and John Leonard moved from Hethe and registered Charles' house as a meeting place. In 1800 (pictured) a chapel was registered on a site in Church Street. In 1827 there were some 400 Dissenters, nearly a quarter of the population. In 1851 they built a new larger chapel, with a gallery, in Chapel Square (Plate 10). In the 1860s they joined Wesleyan Reform and formed the Deddington Wesleyan Reform Circuit. The former chapel served as a Sunday School and a tablet records it as 'Wesleyan Sunday School 1822'; it was sold in the 1990s. By 1857 there were some 1,000 Dissenters, about half the population. In 1895, there were still two Methodist preachers and six

Wesleyan Methodist Chapel, Deddington, built in 1800, later used as their Sunday School (1822 tablet). It is now a private dwelling. © OCC

auxiliaries in the village. The chapel is still active but not on a circuit.

4. *Fritwell*

A house was licensed about 1827. By 1847 a small chapel had been built, possibly on Southfield Lane. In 1874 a new chapel was opened on East Street. It closed in 1920 and is now a private dwelling. In 1892 the Wesleyan Reform Methodist Chapel and Temperance Hall was built on North Street. The chapel is still active and Fritwell is discussed in further detail below (see 3(d)).

5. *Souldern*

Meeting-houses were licensed in 1818/19 but a chapel was not built until 1850. The Wesleyans died out but in 1869 Wesleyan Reformers built a new chapel and in 1873 there were 73 members. The chapel is still active.

6. *Syresham*

In the early 1800s meetings were held in some cottages and friends from Brackley used to attend on a regular basis. A barn, or some cottages, was made into a chapel to accommodate some 50 people. There was considerable opposition and the disturbers sometimes 'captured' the gallery. The present chapel was built in 1846 but only after many attacks on the builders. Later, the deeds of the chapel fell into the hands of one of their opponents, who tried to sell the chapel and its lands over the heads of the trustees. Fortunately, the law intervened to recover the deeds and the chapel remains active to this day. They joined the Reformers some time after 1851.

Closed Chapels

7. *Aynho*

A group were members of the Deddington Circuit in 1879 and there is some evidence that they used to meet in a house off The Square. They never built a chapel.

8. *Barford St Michael*

Various houses were licensed from 1798. A chapel was built in 1840 (pictured). By 1853 the congregation had joined the Reformers. The chapel was closed recently and is now a private residence.

9. *Bodicote*

Methodists were meeting by 1802 but did not build the chapel on East Street until 1845. They joined the Deddington Wesleyan Reform Circuit for a period but left later to join the Banbury Methodist Circuit. They are still active.

10. *Croughton*

The original chapel was built on Chapel Lane in 1829. A new red brick chapel with a stone porch was opened on 27 October 1904. It closed about twenty years ago and is now a private dwelling.

11. *North Aston*

In the early nineteenth century there was a flourishing community of about twenty Methodists with their own meeting-house. By 1860 there were about thirty but they never built their own place of worship. They were still members of the Deddington Circuit in 1879.

12. *Steeple Aston*

A chapel was built on South Side, formerly Chapel Street, in 1852. It was closed in 1968 and became a shop.

13. *Stoke* Lyne

A chapel was never built here. By the 1860s there were few Methodists remaining, although they were still members of the Deddington Circuit in 1879.

Wesleyan Reform Methodist Chapel, Barford St Michael, built in 1840, photo c.1920. It closed recently and is now a private dwelling. © OCC

14. *Whitfield*

A chapel was built about 1823. It closed many years ago and only the railings now remain.

d) Methodist Communities

The great ambition of the Methodists was to build their own chapel. In fifteen cases they never managed to build one, while in twenty-one others they went on to build a larger chapel to replace the first one. In Hornton, for example, when the new Primitive Methodist chapel was opened on 11 May 1885, they must have felt very proud to have it described as 'a more substantial, commodious and altogether more suitable house for divine worship'. A key feature of all their chapels is the central pulpit and reading desk, which serves to emphasise the importance of preaching and readings from the Bible. The interior of Cropredy chapel, which has its original furnishings from 1881, provides an excellent example (Plate 6). In Anglican churches the emphasis is on the chancel and the high altar, with the pulpit off to one side of the nave. This was anathema to the early Puritans, who preferred to hold their services in the nave with a simple table rather than a decorated altar.

Given the dominance of the Methodists in the region, it is time to examine the place and influence of their chapels in the local communities. Fortunately such an examination is helped by the extensive records kept by the Methodists, including monthly preacher plans, schedule books, and records of the various officials and activities involved. The schedule books, among other things, list all the contributions required from members, which include quarterly, chapel and missionary collections. Circuit officers include stewards, and secretaries and treasurers for the various funds, including the W.O.M. Fund (for Worn-Out Ministers!). These records all show how tight central control has been, ever since John Wesley carefully established it before his death in 1791. He formed the Methodist circuits, appointed the itinerant preachers and set up the system of local preachers and regular inspections. Great emphasis was also placed on schools and Sunday schools. The Methodists also extended their influence over leisure, by providing public lectures, evening classes, savings banks, sports and other entertainment, and special services. It is easy to understand why some of them wished to break away from this central control.

In some of the larger villages, like Brailes and Hook Norton, a number of other Nonconformist groups have flourished together with the Methodists. It is in the smaller villages that the Methodists have been dominant. In Hornton, for example, the Primitive Methodists flourished and the Anglican presence briefly almost disappeared, while in Tysoe, unusually, the Wesleyan and Primitive Methodists both flourished and built chapels. In a number of the smaller villages, attendance at one or both of the afternoon and evening services on 30 March 1851 exceeded 100, for example, in Chacombe, Epwell, Sulgrave and Wardington. However, I have selected Fritwell for a closer examination, partly because I have known the village for many years and researched it previously; also because the available records, including oral testimony, do provide an excellent illustration of how the Methodists could influence or even control life in a village community.

Fritwell[11]

In 1852 'Fritwell in the Elms', as it was known, was described as 'expensive and respectable'[12] and the manor was often let for short periods during the hunting season. The quality of the Bicester Hunt was well known and in 1857 the district was described as being 'studded with Gentlemen's Seats and Hunting Boxes, affording society of the most agreeable kind'.[13] The village was also noted for its numerous craftsmen and tradesmen. Unusually for the area, which was very dependent on agriculture, the village did not suffer a sharp decline during the agricultural depressions of the 1870s and 1880s. Indeed, the population rose from 514 in 1851 to a peak of 560 in 1891. There was no dominant squire or family living in the manor in the nineteenth century and no dedicated vicar until the arrival of Samuel York in the 1850s. This seems to have contributed to the rise of Methodism in the village. In spite of this, Fritwell was by no means a typical 'open' village. The quality of many of the eighteenth-century houses on East Street is exceptional and there is no evidence of bad or riotous behaviour. As Flora Thompson wrote of her local Methodists in Juniper Hill, 'Their lives were exemplary', and it seems that Frank Dew (see below) and other Methodist leaders made sure that this was true of Fritwell's Methodists.

In 1829 the premises of Sarah Scott were licensed for a Dissenting Meeting House. By 1847 there was a small chapel, probably in Southfield Lane, off East Street, where the congregation in 1851 was 68 and 84 at the two services. By 1854 there were two 'reformed Methodists' societies, and Cyril Wood, the curate, was commenting that 'The parish in a religious point of view has been thoroughly neglected. Dissenters took the opportunity to establish themselves.' By then, the church was 'in the most disgraceful possible condition and unsafe to minister in'.[14] Frank Dew (see below) also had his own Free Church chapel. In 1874 a new Wesleyan chapel was opened on East

Wesleyan Methodist Chapel, East Street, Fritwell, built in 1874, photographed in the 1920s. It closed in 1920 and is now a private dwelling. © OCC

Street (pictured) with accommodation for about 100. The sermon at the opening contained many references to 'internal dissension', and called for the congregation 'to be united and pull together'.[15] This must have been dissension between members of the Free Church and the mainstream Wesleyans. Shortly afterwards, the Free Church members formed a committee, including Frank Dew and Enos Cox, to build a new chapel on North Street.[16] By 1878 the Methodists were said to form about one-third of the population (i.e. 150-200)[17], although the new Wesleyan Reform Chapel and Temperance Hall on North Street (pictured) was not completed until 1892. Clearly Fritwell had a strong link with the Temperance movement, which 'derived its impetus from the working class, and appealed to the working-class desire for self-dependence, self-education and respectability'.[18] In November 1874, the *Bicester Herald* reported on a Temperance lecture in the Free Church Wesleyan Chapel, and, in November 1881, on Temperance Lodge anniversary services in the Wesleyan Reform Chapel and meetings in Mr Haynes' shed.

No history of Fritwell and its Methodists would be complete without mention of Frank Dew (1840-1901) (pictured) and his partner, Enos Cox. It was they who built the new North Street Chapel in 1892, on land donated by Cox. However, their interests were not confined to chapels. They were serious businessmen and in 1885 they had built the Raghouse Store on East Street for £1,000 (pictured). 'Dew's Groceries, Haberdashery and Ironmongery' was a 'wholesale and retail provider' of almost everything and possibly the largest village store in England at one time. At its peak, there were 22 employees and numerous horse-drawn carts delivering to all the neighbouring villages. Dew's businesses prospered, he became a leading local figure, including secretary of the Fritwell Liberals, and he even used the chapel on East Street for

Wesleyan Reform Methodist Chapel/Temperance Hall, North Street, Fritwell, built in 1892, photographed in 1906. © OCC

extra storage when it closed in 1920. Indeed, you might almost call him the local squire and in 1916 his son George was excused military service, as being 'too important to the local economy'. After Frank Dew's death in 1901, the store was carried on by the Dew family and did not close until the 1970s. It has now been converted into luxury apartments.

Frank Dew was also a key member of the local Methodist community. He had his own chapel, a Free Church one, he was reputed to employ only Methodists, and, like an Anglican squire, he expected his employees to go to chapel. The village had a reputation for the range and quality of its craftsmen and tradesmen. Many of them were Methodists, and there seems to have been a strong network of them living around the store. On Sundays, Dew was a preacher on the local Methodist circuit but, for the rest of the week, he was clearly a very shrewd, and by some accounts, uncompromising, businessman. It was said, for example, that he or one of his staff was likely to be a new mother's first visitor after the midwife, with offers of a pram, cot, and all the essentials for the new baby. There is, however, no suggestion that he would 'adulterate…sugar stocks with sand, and then go down to prayers with …families and assistants', as some Nonconformist grocers were alleged to do![19]

Baptismal and other records for Fritwell show that an overwhelming majority of the Methodists were agricultural labourers with just one or two farmers. Most of the others were carpenters, masons, hurdlemakers, and craftsmen typical of the Fritwell tradition. As we shall see below, most of the chapel trustees, at least initially, also came from this class. This is very much in line with the perception that the overwhelming majority of Nonconformist

'Dew's Groceries, Haberdashery and Ironmongery Store' on East Street, Fritwell, 1904. It closed in the 1970s and has been converted into luxury apartments. © OCC

chapels were made up of the poor, but not the poorest, people, at least until the 1840s. They were also strongly artisan, like Fritwell's Methodists. After the 1840s, it was mainly urban rather than rural Nonconformity that stretched into the lower middle classes.[20]

Services

In 1868 there was an interesting service in the East Street chapel, when 'The Chapel was crowded to excess' to hear a Miss Ghostley preach. George Dew (no relation of Frank), churchwarden at Lower Heyford, admitted that 'Her sermon was very good & to the point. But respecting whether women ought to preach I know not what to say'! The vicar Mr York had warned his church congregation against it; however, 'Many who, before, had never been to Fritwell Chapel went today'.[21] In the same way, most of the local Methodists seem to have been happy to enjoy the variety of

Frank Dew (1840-1901), Fritwell, 1890s. © Wesleyan Reform Methodist Chapel and OCC

Church in the morning and/or afternoon, and Chapel in the evening, as John Wesley would have approved. They brought their fervour to the evening service and appeared to obtain more comfort and support from it than the Church could give.[22] As a clerical commentator on the religious census concluded, 'The morning service may be said to be the service of *necessity*, the afternoon service that of *convenience*, and the evening one that of *devotion*'.[23]

With regard to women preachers, it was generally the Primitive Methodists, not the Wesleyans, who allowed it. However, many of the Fritwell Methodists had already joined Wesleyan Reform and were unlikely to be bound by stricter Wesleyan rules. The itinerant preachers deserve a word here for their major contribution and the huge distances which they covered, mostly on foot, in order to preach at the rural chapels. W.T. Henderson had this comment on a Primitive Methodist preacher, a Mr Brazier, who 'curiously enough was by trade a blacksmith', who attended Charles Spurgeon's sermon in 1857: 'He walked from Banbury to Stratford on Avon 27 miles and then walked back the same distance and preached three times on the Sunday, reaching home at 2 o'clock on the Monday morning'![24]

Both Church and Chapel saw increased attendance in the last forty years of the nineteenth century, and, as Chadwick wrote in his assessment of the late Victorian Church, there was 'a surprising steadiness of church and chapel life'.[25] This certainly seems to have been true of Fritwell. When Bishop Wilberforce came for the rededication of St Olave's Parish Church in June 1865, every farmer, whether Churchman or Dissenter, made a point of being present.[26] If you were aiming for self-improvement and a rise in the world, as Fritwell farmers no doubt were, 'respectability' was an indispensable requirement; attendance at church or chapel would be an obvious start.[27] At the time, there were many Dissenters, 'who sometimes go to one place, sometimes to another'; and in 1866 there were 'only 8 Dissenters who attend chapel and never enter Church'.[28] The chapel is still in active use and a member of the Wesleyan Reform Union, although the congregation, like most in the region, has declined significantly.

Chapel Trustees

The normal pattern of trusteeship of Wesleyan chapels saw the responsibility shared among members of other Wesleyan churches in the Circuit, who were of good standing and capable of bearing the financial responsibility for the chapel.[29] In this respect it is interesting to look at the original trustees for the East Street Chapel in Fritwell in 1872 and a revised list in 1910, fourteen in each case. In 1872 most of the trustees came from local villages, with three from Fritwell, two shopkeepers and a labourer, three from Clifton, the station master, a coal merchant and a labourer, two from Bicester, a Poor Law officer and a baker, two from Brackley, a grocer and a plumber, one from Croughton, a shopkeeper, one from Oxford, a clerk in the Post Office, and two from Upper Heyford, a carpenter and a sawyer. This list shows that the chosen trustees were by-and-large of a better class than most of the Fritwell Methodists, who were predominantly agricultural labourers. In contrast, the new trustees in 1910 were predominantly urban, with two from Bicester, a boot salesman and a builder, three from Brackley, a grocer, a builder and a Temperance Hotel proprietor, six from Buckingham, two drapers, a house furnisher, an ironmonger, a coal merchant, and a Gentleman (Thomas Farwell Roper Hull), and only two from local villages, one from Evenley, a farm bailiff and one from Turweston, a post master. Only one trustee survived from 1872, John Hedges, a baker from Bicester. Again the list shows a desire to recruit a better class of trustee.

A similar pattern emerges in the Wesleyan chapels in other local villages and the same names recur many times, even in a limited survey of nine villages. In Balscote (1890) there were six trustees from Banbury, including a Gentleman, Robert Powell, and three local farmers. In 1898 the trustees included Arthur Fairfax, from the well-known Banbury solicitors Fairfax, Barfield & Blincowe. Like five other Wesleyans between 1889 and 1899, he was mayor of Banbury in 1897 and he also became a trustee for Lower Boddington (1889) and Hinton (1902). In 1935, Harold Barfield, Gentleman of the same firm, was a trustee for Balscote and Hinton, where he was joined by his fellow solicitor, Frederick Blincowe. Upper Boddington (1865) and Wigginton (1883) also ensured that they had a solicitor on board, Thomas Mace, who was Mayor of Chipping Norton by 1885. Upper Boddington also had no less than five farmers. Cropredy (1881) had eight trustees from Banbury, and two members of the Cherry family, William, the carrier, and Thomas, a mason. In 1889, William and Thomas were also trustees for Lower Boddington, where they were joined by John Cherry, a farmer, and George Cherry, a glazier. The Cherry firm of builders, which built the chapel in Cropredy, has been well known for over a hundred years and was based in Cropredy until 2000, when they moved to Great Tew. Another recurring name was Austen or Austin, a family of Quakers from Sibford Gower, who ran a grocery store in George Street, Banbury. Reginald was trustee for Balscote (1898) and Hinton (1902), and Horace for Cropredy (1881).

I also looked at trustees for the Primitive Methodist chapels in Brailes and Hornton. Here there seems to have been less effort or concern to recruit outsiders of good standing. In Brailes in 1863, four of the thirteen trustees were from Banbury, including a coach builder, George Hawkins, and an auctioneer, John Harrison. There was a farmer from Mollington and a tailor from Hornton but the remainder were from Brailes: a coachman, a mason, a gardener, a weaver, and three laborers [sic]. In 1906, eight of the thirteen trustees were from Brailes: a grocer, baker, carrier's assistant, farmer, carpenter, and three laborers. The others were: Thomas Henry Gardner, a well-known farmer from Tysoe, a grocer from Epwell, a cooper from Mollington, and George Percy Stanley, a coal merchant from Hornton, who was manager of the Edgehill Quarries by 1926 and also a trustee for Hornton. In 1927, there were only three outsiders, two farmers from Shipston-on-Stour and the farmer Thomas H. Gardner from Tysoe. There were three farmers and a carpenter from Upper Brailes and two bakers, two draper/grocers, two saddlers and a carrier from Lower Brailes. In Hornton in 1885, two of the fourteen trustees were from Brailes, a grocer and a baker, one from Tysoe, a laborer, and two carpenters, one from Banbury and one from Warmington. The remainder were from Hornton, including a farmer and three laborers, while the rest were tradesmen or craftsmen. In 1926, all thirteen trustees were from Hornton, apart from George Stanley, manager of the Edgehill Quarries. By then there were five farmers and the rest were tradesmen and craftsmen.

Foundation Stones

Apart from appointing trustees for any new chapel, there was also the formal ceremony of laying the foundation stones. It was an honour to be selected to lay one of these stones and have your name inscribed on it. It also appears to have been an accepted custom that this honour should be acknowledged by the gift of £10. There is one name above all others, which appears on these foundation stones, that of William Mewburn (1817-1900) (pictured), for example at Upper Boddington (1865) and Wigginton (1883). He came from a Yorkshire family of Wesleyan Methodists and made a considerable fortune on the Stock Exchange, before moving south in 1865 and buying Wykham Park, near Banbury. Thereafter, he became a great benefactor to all manner of causes but particularly to the Banbury Methodist Circuit, supporting many of its chapels and other buildings. He was also 'especially solicitous for the spiritual as well as temporal well-being of the inhabitants of the poorer rural parishes'.[30] He became High Sheriff of Oxfordshire and later Deputy-Lieutenant. He and his son, William Junior, were trustees of many of the Methodist chapels, sometimes together, for example in Banbury (1884), Grimsbury, Neithrop, Adderbury and Bloxham.

William Mewburn
(1817-1900), 1890s.
© Cheryl Messer

William Senior was also a trustee at Chacombe and Middleton Cheney. One of his four daughters laid foundation stones at Hook Norton in 1875 and at Cropredy in 1881, where her father donated £100, no doubt one of many such donations. William Junior was a trustee at Hinton (1902).

I hope that this chapter has demonstrated the strength of the Methodists, particularly in the nineteenth century, and the powerful influence which they and their chapels could exercise on the local communities. It is now time to examine the other major groups of Nonconformists who were active in the region.

Chapter 4

Baptists

'The Bridge Street church [was] the most influential Dissenting congregation in the town in the late 1850s and early '60s'.[1]

W.T. HENDERSON WAS THE VERY SUCCESSFUL BAPTIST MINISTER at the Bridge Street Chapel from 1851 to 1864. He was a radical, drew huge crowds and was actively involved in local politics as the editor of the Banbury Advertiser, which was founded in 1855 and 'represented the views of militant dissenting radicals'.[2] However, he gave it up after four years, because 'I found it interfered with my Ministerial Work'. It is not surprising that the Baptists were thought to be the most influential Dissenting congregation in Banbury during his ministry. This was against considerable competition, for, as we have seen above (Chapter 2 and Table 5), Dissent of all kinds was flourishing in Banbury in the mid-nineteenth century. Before we look further at the Baptists in Banbury in the nineteenth century, we need to examine their origins.

The Baptist sect was founded in Holland in the early seventeenth century and the first Baptist church in England was founded in 1612 in Newgate Street, London. These were General Baptists, who believed in a General Atonement, and took the view that Christ in his death undertook to make possible the salvation of all men. The Particular (or Strict) Baptists, who were formed in 1633, followed a different theology. They believed, like Calvin, in predestination and took the stricter view that Christ only undertook to save particular individuals, usually referred to as the elect. The majority of early Particular Baptists rejected open membership and open communion. The sect was based initially on seven London churches and their missionary work.

John Bunyan did not share the strict views of the Particular Baptists. When he was released from prison in 1672, he joined the Independent Church in Bedford. The Church tolerated baptism of infants as well as adult believers, like the General Baptists. Some churches moved from Independent to predominantly Baptist. The Bedford church, however, as we have seen, became the Bunyan Meeting Free Church and is now a member of the

Charles Spurgeon speaking at the Music Hall, Royal Surrey Gardens, late 1850s.
© Regent's Park College, Oxford

Congregational Federation as well as the Baptist Union. Many Baptists like to claim Bunyan as their own and, when Bunyan's tomb in Bunhill Fields was restored in May 1862 and he was named 'The Immortal Dreamer', it was the Baptist, Charles Spurgeon, who unveiled it. This shows how the distinction between Baptists and Congregationalists or Independents could be blurred. In Banbury, firm progress towards the formation of Baptist congregations came only when small groups broke away from the Independent church.

In the late seventeenth century, there was steady movement from the General to the Particular Baptists. By 1718 there were only some 19,000 General Baptist 'hearers'. They were relatively strong in Buckinghamshire, Cambridgeshire, Kent and Sussex but weak in urban settings like London and Bristol. They did not generally build chapels for themselves and their decline was almost inevitable. After 1801, there was growing support for Unitarianism. In 1813, a new national organisation was formed, called The General Meeting of the Particular (or Calvinist) Union of Great Britain. In 1815, the Old General Baptist Assembly even passed a resolution affirming that 'Unitarianism, with the exception of baptism, may be surely called the cause of the General Baptists'. In 1873, the national organisation became the Baptist Union.

It was a coup for Henderson in 1857 when Spurgeon accepted his invitation to visit Banbury. By then he was already the most popular preacher of his day. He was pulling in crowds of 10,000 each Sunday at the Surrey Gardens

Music Hall (pictured), round the corner from Clapham Common. On 19 October 1856, there were 10,000 in the streets outside. There was even a rumour that Queen Victoria once appeared at Surrey Gardens in disguise.[3] He had hired the Music Hall while the Metropolitan Tabernacle, near Elephant and Castle, was being built. It was completed in 1861 with seating for some 4,600. It was burned down in 1898 and replaced with a smaller version, which is still in active use. As Chadwick said, it 'owed its building to the young genius, Charles Haddon Spurgeon, who strengthened the impact of dissent and of the Baptists upon the nation'.[4] He believed in open communion, and when he founded a college to train pastors (now called Spurgeon's College), he placed a Congregationalist as its first tutor and later principal.

Charles Spurgeon (1834-92) (Plate 11), who was 'fat, podgy, unimpressive' outside the pulpit, had both amazing gifts as a preacher and also remarkable stamina. On 7 October 1857, on the Indian Mutiny National Day of Prayer, he preached at Crystal Palace to no fewer than 23,654. Were estimates of crowd numbers more accurate in those days? In October 1871, after speaking to thousands at Blackheath, he said 'I spoke 1hr 50min; too long, yet really not long enough for a full development of my points. Physically rather an excess of effort'![5] Not surprisingly, the *Banbury Advertiser* gave full coverage to his visits to Banbury in 1857 and again in 1862, when he attracted about 1,200 to the Bridge Street Chapel. In 1857, as Henderson commented, 'Admission had been by free ticket, and almost every sect was represented, Unitarians, Methodists of all shades, Congregationalists, Hyper-Calvinist and church people'.[6] It certainly supports the view that this was 'the most influential Dissenting congregation in town in the late 1850s and early 1860s'. In 1864, Henderson left Banbury for the prestigious Devonshire Square Church in London, and the influence of the Baptists in Banbury declined.

I stumbled on another interesting link with Spurgeon, and possibly with Bunyan, on a recent visit to Australia. The unusual signpost (Plate 12) in Sheffield, Tasmania, includes directions to the Garden of Eden, Paradise and the Promised Land. These places were given biblical names by Reuben Austin, J.H. Dawson and other Christian Brethren, when they were walking on the foothills of Mt Roland, near Sheffield in the 1870s. It is remarkable that over thirty biblical place names are found here within a few square kilometres, including Zion Hill, Damascus Gate and Devil's Gullet. They immediately conjure up visions of Christian's journey in *Pilgrim's Progress*, which would have been very familiar to these Christian pioneers. They seem to have been devout Calvinists but their leader, Reuben Austin, was apparently fond of reading the published sermons of Charles Spurgeon. Interestingly too, a recent book about the Christian pioneers in Tasmania is titled 'Spurgeon's Men: The Resurgence of Baptist Belief and Practice in Tasmania, 1869-1884'.[7] The influence of Spurgeon and Bunyan clearly spread far beyond the Metropolitan Tabernacle and the Bedford Church. They, and the Christian Brethren in Tasmania, exemplify the enthusiasm and commitment of the various Nonconformist sects.

In the last decades of the nineteenth century, the Baptists and Congregationalists (as Independents were now generally called) were close but never achieved union. As we shall see in the next chapter, it was the Presbyterians and the Congregationalists who finally came together in 1972 to form the United Reformed Church (URC). In general, there is often some difficulty in defining the differences between the various sects, at least until the nineteenth century. There was considerable movement between them, not necessarily on religious grounds. Often it may have been more a procedural or social matter and a question where the individual felt most comfortable with the minister and the congregation. As we know to this day, this can also apply to the Church of England.

It does appear, however, that the Baptists have been the least likely of the Nonconformist sects to participate in any ecumenical movement; their fundamentalism has tended to put the others off. There are few links currently, for example, between 'thepeopleschurch' and other groups in Banbury. Much earlier, in 1833, John Henry Newman wrote to the Rev'd Thomas Mozley from Rome to say 'By this time you are quite at home at Moreton Pinkney (Northants). I wish I had any means of hearing how your Baptist chapel or other stumbling-block are going on; there are no Baptist chapels here'.[8] You can almost hear his sigh of relief that he no longer has to deal with any Baptist chapels. There seem to have been similar problems at the time in nearby Preston Capes. The squire, Sir Charles Knightley, 'was noteworthy because he kept the Nonconformists out of Preston Capes. One of his tenants, a Baptist, held meetings in his house, and when Sir Charles was unable to evict him he had the thatch taken off his roof'![9]

Table 11 shows the Baptist Meetings in Banburyshire 1644-2012. The Banbury Baptist Group of Churches, formed in the 1840s, initially included Banbury Bridge Street and Warwick Road, Hook Norton, Bloxham and Milcombe. In 1971, on becoming part of the District of Oxford and East Gloucestershire, the group expanded to include King's Sutton and Middleton Cheney. Overall, the table does show how the Baptists have been comparatively weak in the region, with only six churches still open. This has allowed the Methodists to achieve a very strong presence.

Table 11		Baptist Meetings in Banburyshire, 1644-2012			
Parish	Population 1851	Premises	Services 30 March 1851 am/pm	Evening	Date of first meeting
Open					
Banbury (Note 1)	4,026	chapel			1971
Bloxham (Note 2)	1,336	chapel	/75	100	1808
Bodicote (Note 3)	673	chapel	/50		pre-1800
Hook Norton (Note 4)	1,496	chapel	100/120		1641
King'sSutton (Note 5)	1,335	chapel (N)	80	116	1781
Middleton Cheney (Note 6)	1,330	chapel (N)	70/130 SS 48/41	45 SS 32	pre-1800
Closed					
Banbury (Note 7)	4,026	chapel	70	50	1738
(Note 8)		chapel	150 SS 50	200	1841
Neithrop (Note 9)	4,180	chapel	70 SS 39/37	77	1834
Barford St Michael (Note 10)	392	chapel	ave 20		1823
Hook Norton(Note 11)	1,496	chapel	100/120 SS 20/20		1773
Little Tew (Note 12)	237	chapel	117		1778
Milcombe (Note 13)	241	chapel	51		1708
N.Newington(Note 14)	436	chapel			1876
Sulgrave (Note 15)	604	chapel (N)	80/150 SS 30	100	1844
Wigginton (Note 16)	314	chapel		35	1835

Notes to Table 11

Open Chapels

1. *Banbury, 'the peopleschurch'*

A new church was built on the site of the old Unitarian Chapel in Horse Fair in 1971 and re-named 'the peopleschurch'. They are strongly evangelical and have attracted large congregations. It is unclear whether they are still members of the Baptist Union.

2. *Bloxham*

From the seventeenth century the Quakers and the Anabaptists were active in Bloxham, Milcombe and Milton. In 1808 Particular Baptists registered a meeting-house, and in 1812 they built a chapel in Bloxham. The vicar described them as 'Calvinistic Baptist Independents'. A Baptist minister was ordained in 1821 and a Sunday School was active by then. A new and larger

Baptist Chursh, Hook Norton, interior, rebuilt in 1781, c. 1920. © OCC.

chapel was built in 1862 (see datestone 'erected in 1862'). The date is confirmed by the *Banbury Guardian* of 24 July 1862, which states that the foundation stone of the new Baptist Chapel will be laid by Mr Ryman of Great Tew on Monday next. Services are now held in Warriners School and other activities in the chapel.

3. *Bodicote*

By 1817 one third of the village was Baptist. The vicar called it 'a conventicle of Anabaptists'. The chapel was sold in 1902 and demolished soon after.

4. *Hook Norton*

The first meeting of the Baptist congregation (Particular Baptists) was held in 1641, one of the oldest in the country. In 1655 an association of seven local churches was established. The first chapel and minister's house were built in 1718, and were rebuilt in 1781 (pictured, also Plate 13). In 1873 a schoolroom in the Gothic style was built where the former almshouses stood. The congregation is still active.

5. *King's Sutton*

From 1781 to 1820 the Baptists met in people's houses, mainly in George

Blake's house which was registered for meetings about 1800. In 1820 his barn was bought and given to the trustees, who fitted it up as a place of worship. Soon after 'a kind of Independent Church was formed' and there was a 'painful period' until a revival of the local Baptists in 1844. A Particular Baptist Church was formed on 12 May 1846 'to be run on Calvinistic principles' but the chapel (Plate 14) was not built until 1867. The manse next door was built in 1892. The congregation is still active.

6. *Middleton Cheney*

A chapel was built in 1806, in lieu of a former small place in another part of the village. It is still active and described as the New Life Community Church.

Closed Chapels

Banbury

7. *Strict Baptists*

Strict Baptists have been recorded in Banbury as far back as 1738. The Strict Baptist chapel was founded in 1829 in West Bar by the ironmonger Joseph Gardner, a member of the Middleton Cheney Baptist chapel. In 1877 these Calvinist Baptists moved to a new chapel on Dashwood Road. It was closed and sold in 1955. There is still a small group of Calvinists meeting on Hanwell Heights.

8. *Particular Baptists*

The Bridge Street Chapel (pictured) was in use by the Particular Baptists from 1841. As we have seen, W.T. Henderson, their minister from 1851 to 1864, was a radical and drew huge crowds, notably when he invited Charles Spurgeon. The chapel was altered in 1903. It closed in 1971, when the Baptists moved to the old Unitarian Chapel in Horse Fair. It became a supermarket about 1975 and only the original chapel façade survives.

9. *Neithrop*

In 1834 Richard Austin, the brewer, built a chapel for the Calvinistic Baptists on the south side of South Bar. They had been meeting on the other side of the road since 1813. The chapel (still known as Austin House) closed in 1851.

Villages

10. *Barford St Michael*

Baptists were meeting in a house from 1823 and a chapel was built in 1838. It was closed in 1890 and became a reading room. It is now the garage of a private house.

11. *Hook Norton*

There is evidence that the Zion Strict Baptists were meeting from 1773. Their chapel was built at a cost of £300 in 1898, in the East End where Windward

Baptist Church, Bridge Street, Banbury, 1841. It closed in 1971. Drawn by Alfred Beesley, c. 1850. © OCC.

House now stands. The site was sold for £1,000 in 1966 and the chapel was demolished in 1968. Under the strict Zion Baptist faith no singing was allowed but there was a harmonium in the chapel.

12. *Little Tew*

A house was registered for the Anabaptists in 1778. A licence was obtained for a chapel in 1829 and it was built c.1845. In 1854 the vicar of Great Tew considered half the population of Little Tew to be Baptists or Ranters. The chapel was rebuilt in 1871 by Robert Ryman (Plate 15). A schoolroom was built in 1925 and sold with the chapel in 1968.

13. *Milcombe*

In 1708 Richard Lovell's house was licensed but the sect is not known. A meeting-house was registered in 1822. A chapel was built in 1824 and rebuilt in 1865 (datestone 1866). The chapel was only two houses away from the Anglican church.

14. *North Newington*

In 1876 a new Calvinistic Baptist chapel was built but it seems to have closed many years ago.

15. *Sulgrave*

A chapel was built in 1844. It is now a private dwelling.

16. *Wigginton*

The Particular Baptists built their chapel, 'of exceptionally severe aspect', near the village hall in 1835. Although the average attendance in 1851 was said to be about 50, by 1854 the rector was able to report that it was 'not very numerously attended'. By 1878 it had long been closed, and it was later used as a store-house.[10]

17. *Horley*

In 1656 Horley was in the lists of the Midland Association of General Baptists, when it was the only such community in Oxfordshire. In 1693 a conventicle in Horley was led by Nathaniel Kinch of Horley, who was licensed to teach at any meeting in the county. It was attended by over 100 people, including gentlemen! No chapel or meeting-house is mentioned and the meeting does not seem to have survived for long.

Plate 1: John Wesley, painted by John Hunter, c.1750. © The Trustees of Wesley's Chapel, City Road, London

Plate 2: Holy Trinity Chapel, Staunton Harold, built in 1653-65. © the author

Plate 3: Moravian Church, Woodford Halse, built in 1906; it closed recently. © the author

Plate 4: Wesleyan Methodist Chapel, Greatworth, built in 1860. © the author

Plate 5: Wesleyan Methodist Chapels, Hinton, the old one on the left built in 1879, the new one on the right in 1902. © the author

Plate 6: Wesleyan Methodist Chapel, Cropredy, interior, built in 1881, showing the importance of the central pulpit, drawn by Hazel Stagg, 2012. © Hazel Stagg

Plate 7: Primitive Methodist Chapel, Little Bourton, built in 1845; it closed in the 1980s. © the author

Plate 8: Primitive Methodist Chapel, Mollington, built in 1845. It closed in 1969. © the author

Plate 9: Primitive
Methodist
Chapel, Ledwell,
built in 1856;
closed in 1954.
© the author

Plate 10: Wesleyan Reform Chapel, Deddington, built in 1851. © the author

Plate 11: Charles
Spurgeon, 1870s.
© Regents Park
College, Oxford

Plate 12: 'Nonconformist' Finger Post, Sheffield, Tasmania. © the author

Plate 13: Baptist Chapel, Hook Norton, rebuilt in 1781, 2010. © Revd John Paul Taylor

Plate 14: Baptist Chapel, King's Sutton, built in 1867. © the author

Plate 15: Baptist Chapel, next to the schoolroom, Little Tew, built in 1871; it closed in 1968. © the author

Plate 16: Independent Chapel, Byfield, built in 1827, it closed in 1999. © the author

Plate 17: Friends Meeting House, Adderbury, with separate buildings on the left for women's and children's meetings, painted by M.F. Thomas, c.1825. © Adderbury and Banbury Meeting

Above left Plate 18: George Fox, etching by William Darton, 1822. © Religious Society of Friends in Britain

Above right Plate 19: Cardinal John Henry Newman, painted by Sir John Everett Millais, 1st Bt., 1881. © National Portrait Gallery, London

Below Plate 20: Friends Meeting-house, Sibford Gower, interior, rebuilt in 1864. © the author

Chapter 5

Congregationalists / Independents

THE CONGREGATIONALISTS, more commonly known earlier as Independents, derived from the Brownists, an early Puritan sect in the sixteenth century. They advocated local congregational control, without any circuit or district organisation like the Methodists and other sects. They also advocated freedom of religion for non-Roman Catholics and the complete separation of church and state. Initially, after the Great Ejection in 1662, this put them at odds with the Presbyterians over state control. In the eighteenth and nineteenth centuries, however, most Presbyterian meetings which remained orthodox came to describe themselves as Congregational. This led to a substantial expansion of the Congregational Church in the early nineteenth century and in 1831 the Congregational Union of England and Wales was founded.

Many of the Presbyterians were wealthy and influential. This was certainly true in Banbury, where it could be said that 'The Presbyterians assembling at the Great Meeting were the aristocrats of Banbury's dissenters'.[1] By 1716 these meetings were held in a meeting-house off Horsefair, 'a vast and ugly converted barn'. Under the leadership of the Cobb family, and supported by many of the town's trading and professional elite, the congregation flourished. In the early nineteenth century, however, Unitarian theology (see Chapter 9) was gradually adopted and by 1830 many of the old Presbyterians, who had not joined the Congregationalists, had 'succumbed to the temptations of Unitarianism'.[2] This move in Banbury seems to have been influenced by Joseph Jevans, the Presbyterian minister at Bloxham. By the 1840s, the Presbyterians were no longer meeting in the chapel off Horsefair and the Unitarians had started meeting in Church Lane.

In 1972 the Congregationalists finally amalgamated with the Presbyterian Church to form the United Reformed Church. As we have seen, the 40th anniversary of this merger coincided with the 350th anniversary of the Great Ejection, so that both were marked at the special service in Westminster Abbey on 7 February 2012. Table 12 shows the Congregational Meetings in Banburyshire, 1669-1990.

Table 12   Congregational/Independent Meetings in Banburyshire
1669-1990

Parish	Population 1851	Premises	Services 30 March 1851		Date of firstmeeting
			am	Evening	
Banbury (Note 1)	8,793	chapel	100	120	1787
Villages					
Adderbury West (Note 2)	370	chapel	51 SS 20/19	120	1828
Byfield (N) (Note 3)	1,021	chapel	100/130 SS 18/21	160	1827
Deddington (Note 4)	2,178	chapel	103 SS 20	123 SS 10	c.1820
Hempton (Note 5)	hamlet	chapel	60 SS 7		c.1800
Gt.Bourton (Note 6)	573	chapel	80		1792
Hornton (Note 7)	591	house	38		1834
Little Kineton (W) (Independent/Baptist)	hamlet (Note 8)	chapel	SS 13	55 SS 13	c.1796
N.Newington (Note 9)	436	chapel	/80	62 SS 31	1832
Shenington (Note 10)	437	chapel	ave 30	ave 55	c.1817
Wroxton (Note 11)	789	chapel		50-60	1820

The old Presbyterians and Unitarians in Banbury presumably attended the Independent chapel in Church Passage. The table, which only includes ten chapels, provides confirmation that the Independents and Congregationalists have never been strong in the region. The last chapel in Banbury, on South Bar, closed c.1990. However, the URC, the former Congregationalists and Presbyterians, still hold their own separate services in St Mary's Church. The last Congregational village church, in Deddington, only closed very recently.

Notes to Table 12

1. *Banbury*

The Presbyterians played a major role in seventeenth-century Dissent in Banbury. In 1787 a group broke away from them and in 1792 they built a chapel in Church Passage. There was a strong Baptist element until they broke away c.1810-12. Joseph Parker (1853-58), a noted zealot, was appointed minister aged 23. He was instrumental in reviving the Independents and moving them to a new church on South Bar in April 1857. The new church, set back on the corner by Banbury Cross, was a Doric oratory with galleries

Left and below. Exterior and interior of the Congregational Chapel, Deddington, built 1881, photographs c.1920. © OCC.

on all four sides. The old chapel was used successively by the Disciples of Christ and the Brethren (Plymouth). The centenary of the South Bar chapel was celebrated in 1956 but it was closed c.1990 and it is now a nightclub called 'The Chapel'!

2. *Adderbury West*

A house was registered in 1828 and a chapel built in 1829 on Cross Hill Road. It was closed in 1955 and sold in 1957. In 1980 it was being used as a warehouse, although a circular plaque still survives.

3. *Byfield*

The Independent Chapel was built in 1827 (Plate 16) but there were many problems in the early years with short-stay ministers. There was a great improvement with the arrival of E.T.Sanders in 1898. He was still there in 1927, when there were 47 members and a thriving Sunday School. In 1851, there were fewer Sunday Scholars than usual 'owing to the intolerance of parties connected with the Established Church'! It closed in 1999 and is now a private dwelling.

4. *Deddington*

a) There was a strong group of Presbyterians here from 1660. Their conventicle met most frequently in a barn in Hempton, which belonged to William Whately, vicar of Banbury. In 1672, he was licensed as a preacher at his house in Deddington.

b) The Independents initially held their meetings in a chapel in a house in the Tchure, off the Market Place, c.1820. It was re-opened in 1846 but sold when it was replaced with a new

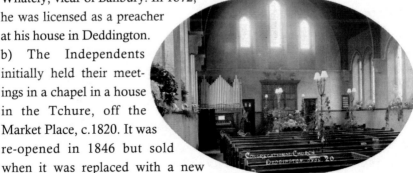

chapel on New Street in May 1881. This impressive new stone chapel was built in Gothic style, with an octagonal east turret. Until recently it was used by the Bible Church from Oxford but it has now closed and been sold for conversion to a private dwelling. On an ecumenical note, the Wesleyan Reform Methodist minister used to take some of their services and some of the congregation have now joined the Reform Chapel.

5. *Hempton*

A hamlet/township in Deddington parish. From 1669 Presbyterian conventicles were held in a barn and in various houses. By 1814 they were said to be attending the Methodist meetings, although by then most of them were Independents. Kelly's Directory of 1924 mentions a Congregational Mission Hall built in 1828 to seat 80 people. An Independent chapel was built in 1876. By 1977 it was a hand-made candle factory.

6. *Great Bourton*

A great variety of Dissent flourished here, with two chapels until 1810. In 1814 the vicar reported that about half the inhabitants were Dissenters, with Antipaedo Baptists, Presbyterians, and Methodists attending the same chapel. There were later moves towards Unitarianism and Congregationalism and there is an 1860 conveyance to Independent trustees. By 1866, it was 'Independent in the morning' and 'anything in the evening'! In 1924, the remaining trustees sold the dilapidated chapel to the Wesleyans, who built a new red brick chapel in 1932. It closed c.2000 and is now the village hall.

7. *Hornton*:

This meeting dates from 1834, although it may be identical with an 'Independent' Methodist meeting held in the 'Bell' in 1854. There is no further mention.

8. *Little Kineton*

A hamlet in Kineton parish. The chapel was built c.1796 for the Independents and Baptists. After 1823, it was usually described as Congregational or Independent. When it was closed and sold in 1895, it was described as Congregational.

9. *North Newington*

In 1832, there was a meeting-house in Broughton parish. In 1837, an Independent chapel was built in North Newington but in 1876 a new Calvinistic Baptist chapel was built.

10. *Shenington*

The Independents shared a chapel with the Primitive Methodists until 1863. By then they had built a chapel on Pertnal Lane but it disappeared quite soon afterwards.

11. *Wroxton*

As early as 1676 Wroxton was home to various Protestant Dissenters, with Quakers, Anabaptists, and Presbyterians listed in various censuses. In 1820 a room was registered for the Independents and a chapel was built in 1823-4 with seating for 200. The chapel disappeared between 1877 and 1883.

Chapter 6

The Society of Friends (Quakers)

THE SOCIETY OF FRIENDS OR QUAKERS was founded by George Fox (1624-91) (Plate 18), who rebelled against the religious and political authorities. He travelled throughout Britain as a dissenting preacher for some 40 years, like John Wesley, and, like him, he was blessed with a powerful voice. He made a number of visits to Oxfordshire, which led to the opening of meeting-houses here, notably the ones in Adderbury and Sibford Gower. He totally repudiated the Calvinist message of election and predestination. 'He welded a disparate band of disillusioned Baptists, former Seekers and near Ranters into one of the most remarkable missionary movements in English history'.[1]

It was in Derby in 1647 that a magistrate, Gervase Bennet, first called Fox and his followers 'Quakers', since they made men 'tremble at the word of God'. The Baptists were the most fruitful recruiting ground for Fox in central and southern England, because many of them found the obsession with baptism and other ceremonies intolerable. There was also the notable conversion of the Leveller John Lilburne towards the end of his life. Before his death in 1657, he was even allowed out of prison on parole to preach for the Quakers. The Quakers suffered persecution more than any other dissenters and a number of them were in Oxford gaol for twelve years, because they would not pay tithes. Fines and goods were also taken from them for holding a conventicle i.e. an illegal assembly. However, many attended church and conventicles, which puzzled Anglican ministers and made it difficult to define a 'dissenter'. It is fairly obvious why they would have been considered subversive at the time. However, it does not follow that they were revolutionaries, as the historian Christopher Hill liked to argue. They were simply delivering a fervent religious message, as John Bunyan also did, and they suffered for it.

The Friends or Quakers (the terms are virtually interchangeable) meet in silence, sometimes called the 'listening silence', seeking guidance direct from the Holy Spirit in their own hearts or through words, which individual Friends may feel called upon to speak. 'The Quaker "Inward Light" linked an individual directly with God, making the prayers and rites of the Church unnecessary'.[2] They have no creed, no sacraments, their children are not baptised, they have no consecrated buildings, they do not sing hymns and have no formal prayers'.[3] Prior to the Act of Toleration in 1689, few Dissenters thought it wise to advertise their presence to possible persecutors by building their own places of worship; they usually settled for a barn or rented room. The 'ever reckless' Quakers, however, built their own meeting-houses throughout the reign of Charles II and rebuilt them when they were pulled down.

The first half of the eighteenth century saw a decline in most branches of Dissent. The Quakers were not immune and there were complaints of 'coldness of zeal' in 1731, 'declension and remissness' in 1741, and 'diverse evils to the dishonour of truth' in 1748.[4] The evangelical confrontational years of George Fox were over and their mission was now largely to other Quakers. As early as 1696, the Bristol Yearly Meeting cautioned Friends to avoid 'disputings and public contentions with wrangling persons'. What would Fox have thought! The emphasis was now on the virtues of plain speech and plain dress, and less on conversion of the world. By 1750, it was estimated that 'between 80 and 90 per cent of Quakers were themselves the children of Friends'.[5] 'Eighteenth-century Quakers came to place great emphasis on silent meetings, spoken ministry became the exception rather than the rule,' and they lost their original evangelical zeal.[6] In the first half of the nineteenth century, they lost members to Baptists, Congregationalists, Plymouth Brethren and Low Church Anglicans. Later in the century, when there was growth for mainstream Nonconformity – Methodists, Baptists, Congregationalists – there was decline for the Quakers and Unitarians.[7]

The Quakers do not have a circuit like the Methodists. However, for a district there has been, for well over 300 years, a 'Monthly Meeting', which oversees a number of local meetings. There are also 'General Meetings' which cover wider areas. Finally, there is the 'Yearly Meeting', which is the national body in London. Table 13 lists the Quaker Meetings in Banburyshire 1654-2012. It shows that all the Meetings started in the late seventeenth century and most of them built a meeting-house in this period. Only the ones in Banbury, Adderbury and Sibford Gower are still active.

Notes to Table 13
Open Meeting-houses

1. *Banbury*

The first Quaker meetings were held in 1654 and there were regular meetings in 1655 in private houses. Banbury Meeting headed one of three Divisions in the

Table 13		Quaker Meetings in Banburyshire, 1654-2012		
Parish	Population 1851	Services 30 March 1851 am	pm	Date of first meeting
Open				
Banbury	8,793	60	39	1654 Note 1
West Adderbury	370	16		1675 Note 2
Sibford Gower	549	112		c.1670 Note 3
Closed				
Barton (Middle)	757			c.1700 Note 4
Brailes (W)	1,284	ave 8		c.1670 Note 5
Eydon (N)	621	13		1691 Note 6
Hook Norton	1,496	11		1668 Note 7
North Newington	436			1665 Note 8
Shutford	416			1668 Note 9
South Newington	419			1692 Note 10
	N = Northamptonshire, W = Warwickshire			

county. In 1657 the first meeting-house was opened behind the Flower de Luce Inn in Broad Lane. The present meeting-house on North Bar was built on the site bought in 1664. It was re-built in 1748-50 and a Tuscan porch was added c.1820. The Meeting is still active, as part of the Banbury and Evesham Area Meeting.

2. *Adderbury West*[8]

In 1675 Bray D'Oily built the meeting-house on his East House estate (next to the present Katharine House Hospice). It was formally opened by George Fox, who had visited D'Oily from 1673 to 1675. It was designed to accommodate 102 men on the ground floor and 60 women in the gallery (known as the loft by the Quakers). The meetings became so popular that two small cottages were built in front of the meeting-house for the women's meetings (Plate 17). They were also used at times to house poor Quaker families.

During the Second World War, an evacuee family stayed in the meeting-house throughout the war, without any water or electricity! After many years of neglect and little use, the building has been fully, and sympathetically, restored. It has a magical atmosphere and the Banbury and Evesham Meeting still use it regularly. Additional cottages were built on the site in the 1680s and were used for women's meetings and for housing some of the poor. The buildings were all used for evacuees in the Second World War. The cottages were demolished in the 1950s.

3. *Sibford Gower*

A small meeting-house was built in 1681, following a visit by George Fox in 1678. It was rebuilt in 1864 (pictured, also Plate 20) 'to meet an increasing demand from

Friends Meeting-house, Sibford Gower, rebuilt 1864, photo 1906. © OCC

the proximity of the Friends' school at Sibford Ferris'.[9] Until the Methodist chapel was completed in 1827, this seems to have been the only place of worship in the Sibfords. Unusually, it was not until 1840 that the Anglican Church of the Holy Trinity in Sibford Gower was built. Until then the Sibfords were included in the Parish of Swalcliffe. As Leslie Baily, a long-time resident, commented, 'A pioneering or dissenting spirit runs like a silver thread through the history of the Sibford villages and Sibford School'. Inside the meeting-house there used to be a partition, which could be lowered to separate men and women. In 1890, some of the panels from it were used in building the Mission Room next door. The Meeting is still active.

Closed Meeting-houses

4. *Middle Barton*

Quaker Cottage used to be two cottages. The further one was used as a meeting-house from the early 1700s until 1856.

5. *Brailes*

Their meeting-house was said to have been erected in the time of George Fox. By 1880 it was being used by the Wesleyans.

6. *Eydon*

A house was registered in 1691 and a meeting-house was built c.1701. It closed in 1868.

7. *Hook Norton*

The first meeting was held in 1668. In 1705 a meeting-house was built in Southrop, next to Southrop House. The Meeting was discontinued in 1888. The Primitive Methodists had part use from 1851 to 1898 and they maintained the building. There was occasional use by the Quakers after 1888, until the meeting-house was demolished in 1932.

8. *North Newington*

There were active meetings from 1665 into the nineteenth century. George Fox visited in 1668.

9. *Shutford*

The first meeting was held in 1668. The meeting-house in Ivy Lane, now called Quaker Cottage, was built in 1689. In the seventeenth century there were 17 Quaker families, in the eighteenth century 23 and in the nineteenth century just five. In 1786 the Shutford Society merged with Banbury.

10. *South Newington*

The meeting-house was built in 1692 (see datestone) but leased to the Primitive Methodists from 1857 until they built their own chapel in 1875. The Meeting closed in 1804 and the burial ground closed in 1851. The meeting-house is now used as the village hall.

Chapter 7

Roman Catholics

'folks as prays to images'... 'they also worshipped the Pope, a bad old man, some said in league with the Devil'.[1]

APART FROM SOME GREAT CATHOLIC FAMILIES, like the Talbots at Heythrop and the Fermors at Tusmore Park, the local Catholics were mainly working-class and mainly Irish. Most of them came over in the nineteenth century to help with building the railways or with the harvesting on the farms. In Lark Rise 'the Catholic minority at the inn was treated with respect, for a landlord could do no wrong'. However, 'On Catholicism at large, the Lark Rise people looked with contemptuous intolerance, for they regarded it as heathenism, and what excuse could there be for that in a Christian country?' The children 'were told they were "folks as prays to images" and "worshipped the Pope", and yet 'the children's grandfather, when the sound of the Angelus bell was borne on the wind from the chapel in the next village (Hethe), would take off his hat and, after a moment's silence, murmur, "In my Father's house are many mansions". It was all very puzzling'.[2]

Later, when Flora was working at the Post Office, she describes how she helped some of the Irish farm workers to write home to their wives. Most of the older ones could not write, so they dictated the letters. Flora noticed that 'there were none of the long pauses usual when she was writing the occasional letter for one of her own old countrymen. Words came freely to the Irishman, and there were rich, warm phrases in his letters that sounded like poetry...The Irishman, too, had better manners. ... The younger men were inclined to pay compliments, but they did so in such charming words that no one could have felt offended'.[3]

This was all in the nineteenth century. Much earlier, a small number of Catholics were meeting in the region from the late sixteenth century. They were known as recusants for refusing to attend their parish church. They must have hoped for greater freedom when Charles II returned in 1660, because his desire for toleration was recognised and he was also thought to be a closet

Catholic. However, in spite of his good intentions and promises, he was unable to convince the Cavalier Parliament, which was determined, in particular, not to tolerate the Presbyterians. They also continued to persecute the Catholics, excluding them from civil and military office and then from Parliament. Full emancipation did not come until 1829, although it was not until 1871 that Catholics were allowed to take university degrees or hold office in universities. Needless to say, they all felt 'a great sense of separateness'.

The local story would not be complete without some mention of Oxford and England's greatest Catholic, John Henry Newman (1801-90) (Plate 19), who was also one of the greatest Englishmen of the nineteenth century. There may be no record of him visiting Banbury but he was a regular visitor down the road at Deddington to hear two famous preachers in the 1820s: Richard Greaves (an Evangelical and later a Unitarian) and his curate, John Hughes. In 1845 he converted to the Catholic faith and moved to Birmingham, where in 1848 he founded the Oratorian Congregation. However, the present impressive Oratory Church was not opened officially until 1909. Newman was made a Cardinal in 1879. By chance, I stumbled on a remarkable letter from Newman in the Banbury Guardian of 3 July 1862 (see Appendix). It had been published originally in The Globe (a London evening paper) on 30 June 1862. In the letter Newman refutes a rumour in the previous day's paper that he might be returning to the Church of England. In very strong language he confirms his loyalty to the Catholic Church and the Pontiff. In even stronger language he rejects Protestantism, which he declares to be 'the dreariest of possible religions'. He continues, 'the thought of the Anglican services makes me shiver, and the thought of the Thirty-nine Articles makes me shudder. Return to the Church of England! No; "the net is broken and we are delivered." I should be a consummate fool (to use a mild term) if in my old age I left "the land of milk and honey" for the city of confusion and the house of bondage'. His rejection of the Anglicans could hardly have been any stronger. However, it has been said that he was too Anglican for the Catholics but too Catholic for the Anglicans.

There had been great public excitement nationally and locally in 1845 when Newman 'went over to Rome', and it led to the founding of the Banbury Protestant Institute. It was a largely Anglican body, which organised a programme of lectures in defence of the Church. There was a significant Catholic congregation in Banbury by the 1840s and fear of the Church of Rome led to some very outspoken opposition in the town. It is no surprise therefore that this letter from Newman was reprinted in the Guardian; it would have been of great local interest. Table 14 lists the Catholic Meetings in Banburyshire 1577-2012 and shows how few Catholics there have been in the region. In 1851 just eight Catholic parish priests responded to the religious census in Oxfordshire and only six in Northamptonshire. Today, there are just seven churches and chapels open in the region, although it should be noted that St John's in Banbury has received a boost with the influx of Catholics from Poland. Of the surviving churches and chapels, the one in Brailes, which dates from 1726, merits a particular mention; it is a very special place (see below).

Table 14		Catholic Meetings in Banburyshire, 1577-2012			
Parish	Population 1851	Premises	Services 30 March 1851 am/pm	Evening	Date of first chapel or church
Open					
Banbury (Note 1)	8,793	St John's	250	230	1838
(Note 2)		St Joseph			1968
Adderbury W.(Note3)	370	church			1956
Brailes(W) (Note 4)	1,284	chapel	130/80		1726
Hethe (Note 5)	418	chapel	150		1832
Kineton (W) (Note 6)	1,023	church			1922
Wroxton (Note 7)	789	chapel			1887
Closed					
Deddington (Note 8)	2,178	house			C17
Heythrop (Note 9)	190	chapel	63	14	1826
Hook Norton (Note 10)	1,496	chapel			1932
Souldern (Note 11)	619	chapel			1869
Woodford Halse (Hinton) (N) (Note 12)	800	church			1912
N = Northamptonshire, W = Warwickshire					

Notes to Table 14
Open Churches and Chapels
Banbury
1. St John's

A chapel was opened in Overthorpe in 1806. St John's Church in South Bar was opened in 1838 (pictured). About 1950 the church had the second most active members in the town.

2. St Joseph the Worker

In 1965 the Church of St Joseph the Worker opened in Edmunds Road, Bretch Hill, as a chapel of ease for St John's Church. It became the centre of a separate parish in 1968. St Thomas of Canterbury in Wroxton is in the same parish.

St John's Roman Catholic Church, Banbury, built 1838, photo 1878. © OCC

Villages

3. *Adderbury West*

There was a considerable Catholic community in the twentieth century before any chapel was built. Mass was said in private houses, notably Court End, where the dowager Lady Bedingfield converted a garden-room into a chapel. In 1956 St George's Chapel was built, 'a hut-like structure run up with economy in mind, which has been compared not inaptly to an electricity sub-station'. In 1984 Adderbury was joined to Hethe to create the new parish of Hethe-with-Adderbury.

4. *Brailes[4]*

'Catholic Brailes is distinguished both for its continuity and as the birth place of William Bishop (1554-1624), the first Catholic Bishop after the Reformation'. From 1535, the Bishop family lived at Rectory Farm, Friars Lane, where they had a secret mass centre with two hiding-holes for priests. They also supported a Catholic school which sometimes had to be of a clandestine nature. The last Catholic school in Friars Lane closed in 1953. The present chapel, constructed in the old malt-barn at Rectory Farm, was opened to the public in 1726. This was a brave act since the laws prohibiting the Mass were not repealed until 1778 and those allowing it to be offered in Registered Chapels not passed until 1791.

The chapel (pictured) is almost under the lee of St George's but no one ever betrayed them. It is also notable that Father John Austin, Pastor to the Catholics from 1785 to 1809, is buried in St George's and there is a tablet in

Roman Catholic Chapel, Brailes, interior, built 1726, photo c.1920. © OCC.

his memory on the exterior wall. This is certainly an example of the great ecumenical spirit which has existed in Brailes. The chapel was subsequently enlarged. It must be said that it is a very special place, entered as it is 'by a flight of stone steps (well concealed) and aptly reminding us of the upper room set out for the Last Supper'. In 1973 the three parishes of Brailes, Shipston and Ilmington were combined to form the parish of Our Lady and the Apostles.

5. *Hethe*

Catholic recusants were meeting in the area from the late sixteenth century, with a priest resident at Tusmore until 1810. The chapel furniture was then moved to the Old Manor House (now Manor Farm), where a chapel was made in the barrel vaulted attic. In 1810 Father Samuel Corbishley took charge of the Mission in Hardwick. He was a very strict and austere priest and he lived in Hardwick until his death on 25 December 1830, serving a flock of some 350, and also keeping a small school. There is a plaque in his memory in St John's Church in Banbury, where he is buried. In 1830, immediately after his death, the Hardwick Manor House was closed to Catholics and Father Alfred McGuire was appointed. He lived in Hethe and rapidly organised land and subscriptions for a new church. Holy Trinity Church (pictured), which was one of the first to be built after the Catholic Emancipation Act of 1829, opened on 22 May 1832 and continues to flourish to this day. As noted above, in 1984 Adderbury was joined to Hethe to create the new parish of Hethe-with-Adderbury.

Holy Trinity Roman Catholic Chapel, Hethe, interior, built 1832, postcard early 1960s.
© Mary Morgan.

6. *Kineton*

St Joseph's Catholic Church in Avon Dassett was built in 1855, as the parish church for a wide area including Kineton. It remained the parish church until 1971 but by 1922 it was decided to build an additional church, St Francis of Assisi, in Kineton. A barn was converted on the east side of Bridge Street. In 1971 the Presbytery was moved from Avon Dassett to Market Square, Kineton. A new church was completed on the site in 1975 and is still active.

7. *Wroxton*

The old chapel at Wroxton Abbey, which was the site of an Augustinian Priory, has some fine woodwork from the sixteenth and seventeenth centuries and a unique little gallery with fine carved panels. In 1681 the North family came into possession and in 1747 the chapel was remodelled in the Gothic style by Sanderson Miller. The chapel was used by the family until a Mission was established in 1883. In 1887 the Norths built a new chapel, St Thomas of Canterbury on Silver Street, which they presented to the village in 1894. It is in the same parish as St Joseph the Worker in Banbury and it is still active.

Closed Churches and Chapels

8. *Deddington*

A small Catholic community survived into the nineteenth century.

9. *Heythrop*

There was a Catholic chaplain at Heythrop House by 1739 but a chapel was

Roman Catholic Church, Heythrop, 1826, demolished 1880. © OCC

not licensed until 1826 (pictured). The chapel was demolished in 1880 and the materials were used in building a new parish church.

10. *Hook Norton*

In 1932 a wooden chapel was built on Rope Way, Southrop. It was closed in 1997 and demolished.

11. *Souldern*

In the sixteenth century the village was an important early stronghold for Catholic recusants in the area. In the eighteenth century there was a chapel in the attic of the manor house. It ceased to be used for worship in 1781 but was reopened in 1852 by Dr J.T. Dolman. In 1869 Mrs J.J. Dolman erected the Chapel of St Joseph in the grounds of Souldern House. In 1871 there were 39 Catholics and at the end of the century some nine families. It must have closed by 1914. In 1956 St Christopher's Chapel was established at the Upper Heyford Air Force Base, in Souldern parish. This closed when the Americans left in the early 1990s.

12. *Woodford Halse (Hinton)*

A small Catholic church, opposite the Methodist chapel, was provided in Hinton in 1912 to serve the parish and the neighbouring villages. It closed about 2008.

Chapter 8

Chapel and Community

'In the vigorous spring of Victorian energy all religions flourished as never before,' and there was also 'a surprising steadiness of church and chapel life in the country'.[1]

IF THE RELIGIOUS SCENE IN THE LATE NINETEENTH CENTURY was apparently so peaceful, it raises the question as to what were the real distinctions within what has sometimes been called the 'mixed bag' of Nonconformity. Were they theological or more to do with class and social distinctions, the local minister, and what was on offer in a particular village? As we have seen, the distinctions in the seventeenth and eighteenth centuries were by no means clear-cut, for example between the Baptists and Independents. In Banbury, firm progress towards the formation of Baptist congregations came only when small groups broke away from the Independent church. Similarly, John Bunyan joined the Independent Church in Bedford in 1660. However, when the church moved to Mill Lane in 1672, it became the Bunyan Meeting Free Church. The Meeting has continued to worship there under this name to the present day and it is a member of both the Congregational Federation and the Baptist Union, and an observer at the United Reform Church (URC). Bunyan himself never wanted to be pigeon-holed, even if the Baptists tend to claim him!

Locally, we have seen in Great Bourton how about half the inhabitants were Dissenters, with Antipaedo Baptists, Presbyterians, and Methodists all attending the same chapel, and later moves towards Unitarianism and Congregationalism. By 1866 the rector reported that it was 'Independent in the morning' and 'anything in the evening'. In Deddington, the remaining Congregationalists have moved over to the Wesleyan Reform Chapel after their own chapel closed. These and other examples show how people could move easily from one sect to another, influenced perhaps more by the minister in charge or by social factors rather than by their religious convictions. As a recent Anglican convert to Catholicism was quoted as saying 'I didn't really analyse a great deal. I just felt more at home there'. This may well have been true of many Nonconformists, and, as many of us are aware, the Church of England is not immune to similar experiences.

It is clear that, within Dissent itself, there were social distinctions. 'At the top of the scale, and very definitely above the lower middle class, came the Unitarians, mainly because of their intellectual standing'.[2] The Quakers and Presbyterians were also felt to be socially superior. In Norfolk the Quakers had the Gurney, Barclay and Buxton families and in York, the Rowntree family, while Birmingham had seven Quaker mayors before 1892. 'The Methodists were not far below them but the split branches of the Methodists veered towards the lower end; and the lowest rung of all was occupied by the Congregationalists and the Baptists'.[3] The Wesleyans were mainly lower middle class and artisans. Although no women ministers were permitted, some did become eminent local preachers. Did Miss Ghostley of Fritwell fame achieve such eminence? Some of the women chose to stand within the communion rail and not in the pulpit when they preached. The 'Prims' were generally working class, 'the simple folk', and below the Wesleyans, and they did use women as ministers.

The Congregationalists and Independents were a veritable 'mixed bag' on their own, absorbing many of the Puritan Presbyterians and later becoming part of the United Reformed Church. They seem to rank below the Wesleyans. The Baptists were also a 'mixed bag' and generally lower class than the Congregationalists, like the relationship between the Wesleyan and Primitive Methodists. Finally, there were the Roman Catholics, with a deep social divide between the top and the bottom. There were the great families, like the Talbots at Heythrop, 'in their indigenous strongholds, proudly and aloofly aristocratic'; among the rank and file (mainly Irish immigrants) the lowest of the labouring class, with many destitute. Until the influx of the Anglican converts in the 1840s and 1850s, English Catholicism was a social anomaly. It had no middle'.[4]

The Chapels

It was the ambition of all the Nonconformists to build their own chapel or meeting-house. We have already seen the strength of the Methodists in the region and looked at the influence of the chapel on their lives and the local communities. This strength is confirmed by Table 15 below, which shows the Dates of Nonconformist Chapels and Meeting-houses in Banburyshire, 1662-1992. The impressive total of 142 chapels and meeting-houses, including 27 replacements for the original buildings, is a tribute to the enthusiasm and

Table 15   Dates of Dissenting Chapels, Meeting-houses and Catholic churches in Banburyshire, 1662-1992   (Note 1)

Date	Wesleyan (Note 2)	Primitive Methodist	Baptist	Independ't	Quaker	Catholic	Total
1662					1		1
1670s					2		2
1680s					2		2
1690s					1		1
1700-50			1		2	2	5
1790s	2			2			4
1800-09	4	1	1				6
1810-19	7		2				9
1820s	8		2	2		1	13
1830s	2	3	3	1		2	11
1840s	8	6	3	1			18
1850s	7	6					13
1860s	3	6	1	1		1	12
1870s	2	2	1	1			6
1880s	1			1			2
1890s	1		1				2
1910-25						2	2
1930s	3					1	4
1950s	1					1	2
1960s						1	1
1970s			1				1
1990s	1						1
	50	24	16	9	8	11	118
Replacements (Note 3)	20	1	3	2		1	27
Total Built	70	25	19	11	8	12	145
Open in 2012	24	0	5	0	3	7	39

Notes to Table 15

1. The table shows the dates of the 118 first chapels, meeting-houses, and Catholic churches. In most cases groups were meeting well before a chapel, meeting-house or Catholic church was built. In 19 cases the congregations never managed to erect a separate building.

2. The Wesleyan chapels include those which transferred to Wesleyan Reform sometime after 1859.

3. Most of the 27 replacement chapels were built between 1850 and 1900.

persistence, even courage, of those involved. The table shows that 77 of these chapels were built between 1820 and 1910, the majority of them before 1870. The Methodists alone built 95 (61%) of the 145 chapels, and 24 (61%) of the 39 chapels still open are Methodist. It was said that at one point in the nineteenth century a new Methodist chapel was being opened every week. In this connection, it is worth mentioning that in 1881 the new chapel in Cropredy was built in about four months! In most of the local villages the Methodists were in the ascendant and only three of the fifty-five parishes with Nonconformists in our survey did not have a Methodist chapel or meeting-house at some point: in Broughton there were Independents in the neighbouring hamlet of North Newington, in Great Tew there were Baptists in the chapelry of Little Tew, and in Heythrop there were Roman Catholics. It is beyond my knowledge and remit to compare the building of chapels in Banburyshire with other areas of England. However, the number of Methodist chapels here is certainly impressive and must bear comparison with some of their most successful areas, for example, the Midland cities and the South West. Sadly, a number of the rural chapels have closed recently and the Goodman Methodist Chapel in Wroxton seems likely to close in the near future.

Community Life

(a) Banbury

The Nonconformist scene in Banbury, particularly in the nineteenth century, was very different from that in the villages and much more political. The Baptist minister, W.T. Henderson, for example, was so politically involved that he became editor of the *Banbury Advertiser*. This was not unusual for a Nonconformist. 'The late eighteenth and first half of the nineteenth centuries saw a vast increase in the numbers of newspapers and magazines published, and a significant proportion of those publications were owned and edited by Nonconformists'.[5] The late nineteenth century saw the growth of 'respectability' and political influence of the Nonconformists. In Banbury this was particularly true of the new Marlborough Road Methodist Church, built in 1865. It became fashionable, its congregation was rich and it dominated the social and political scene. As we have seen, there were six Wesleyan mayors of Banbury in the period 1889-99. The Marlborough Road Church seems to have become somewhat arrogant and removed from the poor in this period. This was very much an urban phenomenon, while rural congregations remained more connected with the working class and the poor.

Nationally, the peak of Nonconformist influence came in 1906, the year of the great Liberal landslide, when nearly half of the 401 Liberal MPs elected were Nonconformists. Thereafter, their political influence may have declined, although it is worth mentioning that Neville Chamberlain, Prime Minister 1937-40, was the son of a former Unitarian mayor of Birmingham, and that even in the 1980s the leaders of the Conservative and Labour parties (Margaret Thatcher and Michael Foot) were the products of Methodist homes.[6]

Table 5 above shows that there were at least fifteen places of worship in Banbury during the nineteenth century, and today there are at least twenty-three (see Chapter 9)! The 1851 religious census for Banbury and Neithrop recorded no less than nine Dissenting options. The Wesleyans were by far the strongest numerically but Dissent was at its height in the town. Clearly the Baptists under Henderson were also extremely popular and he was drawing huge crowds, particularly when Charles Spurgeon came to preach. There were stormy relations between some of the sects, mainly Independents of various kinds. In general, however, we hear little of religious controversy in the late Victorian period and there seems to have been more friendship between the Church of England and Dissent. In his assessment of the Victorian Church in this period, when Nonconformity was flourishing, Chadwick felt able to state that 'In the vigorous spring of Victorian energy all religions flourished as never before', and that there was also 'a surprising steadiness of church and chapel life in the country'.[7] This seems to have been true of Banbury.

(b) The Villages

There is evidence that relations in the villages between the various sects and with the Church of England have also generally been peaceful and tolerant. This is borne out by the experience in Fritwell, where both church and chapel attendance increased in the last forty years of the nineteenth century. The father of Joseph Arch, the founder of the Agricultural Labourers Union, may have been typical of farm labourers in this period. He was regular in church attendance, and his son wrote of him, 'I suppose he kept on going because he had always been accustomed to go, so to church he went'.[8] The young Joseph Ashby of Tysoe was a similar case: 'He accompanied his mother to church in the morning but claimed freedom to wander in the evenings, visiting the "Primitive" and "Wesleyan" chapels in Tysoe and sometimes going off across the fields to chapels and churches in other villages: only religious adventure and exploration was allowed on Sundays'.[9] However, relations with the Church depended very much on the attitude of the local rector and squire. In some cases their opposition to any dissent could be very powerful, for example, Lord Saye and Sele's violent opposition to the Quakers in Broughton in the late 1650s, which forced them out into neighbouring North Newington. There was a similar, if less violent, attitude in Cottisford in the late nineteenth century, when you can sense the relief of Charles Harrison, the rector, in writing that 'the greatest unity prevails from almost the absence of dissent'.[10] The few dissenting Methodists met in the neighbouring hamlet of Juniper Hill. In general it was expedient for many poor people to go to church, since their cottages were tied to their employment. The squire and the rector expected deference and attendance at church. As Henry Peck of Eydon often said, 'A man's a fool if he don't keep in with the folk with money'.[11] This was said in the nineteenth century but it still made good sense much later, even in the mid-twentieth century.

In twenty-five of the parishes in our survey there were at least two Dissenting options. In four of them there were more than two options: Adderbury, Brailes, Hook Norton and Middleton Cheney, all of them larger villages with populations well in excess of a thousand. Even there relations seem to have been generally peaceful. In Brailes, as we have seen, the village was said to have always been very ecumenical. 'There are very good relations and sometimes joint services between the Roman Catholic, Methodist and Anglican churches. Curiously, the Catholic family of Bishop exercised the patronage of the Anglican Church for 150 years, after Elizabeth I, always anxious for money, disposed of it to John Bishop in 1584'.[12] Unusually, there is also a tablet on the exterior wall of St George's Anglican Church in memory of the Catholic Pastor, Fr John Austin, who died in 1809. In Hook Norton, in 1851, there were Wesleyans, 'Prims', Baptists and Quakers, as well as a strong Anglican church. There was also a Zion Strict Baptist chapel from 1898 to 1966 and the Catholics built a chapel in neighbouring Southrop in the 1930s. Unusually, it has been the Baptists of Old Dissent who have survived in Hook Norton, while the Methodists, Quakers and others no longer meet in the village. The Baptist congregation is one of the oldest in the country, having first met in 1641.

Ecumenical Movements

The prime current example of an ecumenical movement in Banbury is St Francis Local Ecumenical Partnership (LEP), which meets on Highlands. An ecumenical group used to meet in that area in the late 1980s. The Roman Catholics bought the land on Highlands for an ecumenical church, which was built in 1992. There were five partners initially: Anglicans, Methodists, Roman Catholics, the United Reform Church (URC) and the Southam Brethren (Evangelicals). The Brethren are now sleeping partners and continue their individual worship on the corner of Cope Road and the Southam Road. An extension to St Francis is planned for a Sunday School, with most of the £130,000 cost already raised. The LEP services follow the format of the presiding minister and they use the Methodist Hymns and Psalms and the Songs of Fellowship. There are services with the Roman Catholics twice a month. They maintain close links with the Marlborough Road Methodists and with St Mary's Anglican Church but not with the Baptists. David Jackson, their recently retired minister, lived next door to the church. Interestingly, he was a Wesleyan minister but became an Anglican one later, with what he calls 'the episcopal element' added. It is because this element is not included in Methodist ordination that the Church of England does not recognise it. A covenant has been signed in the last ten years between them but union seems unlikely in the near future.

There is a further example of ecumenical progress at St Mary's Anglican Church on South Bar. The Anglicans and the United Reform Church (URC) have come together to form 'St Mary's Anglican and United Reform Church'. This allows the URC, the former Congregationalists and Presbyterians, to hold its own separate services in the church. Apart from these examples, there seem to be limited ecumenical initiatives in Banbury, although there is no evidence that relationships between the various sects are unfriendly. There are certainly some initiatives in the local parishes: in Hornton-with-Horley there is an LEP between the Methodists and the Church of England, and in Cropredy a New Worship and Fellowship ecumenical meeting in the Methodist Church. In the Shelswell Benefice, near Bicester, the Anglicans hold joint services with the Roman Catholics of Hethe-with-Adderbury, and in Bicester a new ecumenical church has been built in Bure Park. These initiatives seem to offer some hope for further progress against the rise of secularism.

Chapter 9

Other Groups and Movements

WE HAVE NOW LOOKED AT ALL THE MAJOR BRANCHES of Nonconformity which have been active in the region. There are some other lesser groups and movements, which have also been active, particularly in Banbury. Their presence in the villages is not so easy to determine. The numbers involved may have been small but their influence in some cases has been disproportionate, for example the Unitarians in Banbury. The current list of advertised places of worship in the town provides an interesting starting point and comparison to the nineteenth century.

Places of Worship in Banbury

Table 5 showed that there were at least fifteen different denominations or sects in Banbury in the nineteenth century. As W.T. Henderson said in 1857 'we pretty well had them all. Indeed, it had been said that if a man lost his religion, he might well find it in Banbury'. The current variety of regular religious meetings in Banbury suggests that you could say the same today. It certainly seems to cater for all tastes, which lends support to the argument that Banbury has always been in some way separate and different from other towns. The following twenty-three places of worship are regularly listed in the *Banbury Guardian*:

1   St Mary's Church, Horse Fair.
2   St Paul's Church, Warwick Road.
3   St Leonard's Church, Grimsbury.
4   St Hugh's Church, Ruskin Road.
5   St Francis Church, Local Ecumenical Partnership, Highlands.
6   Easington Methodist Church, Grange Road.
7   Fairway Methodist Church.
8   Marlborough Road Methodist Church.
9.   Grimsbury Methodist Church, West Street, shared with Grimsbury

Baptist Church.

10 Neithrop Methodist Church, Boxhedge Road.

11 thepeopleschurch, Horse Fair.

12 Religious Society of Friends (Quakers), Horse Fair.

13 Banbury Buddhist Group, Quakers' Meeting House, Horse Fair.

14 Banbury Community Church, Broughton Hall, Banbury School.

15 Banbury Evangelical Free Church, Lecture Theatre, Banbury School.

16 Jubilee Church, Rotary Way, Hanwell Fields Community Centre.

17 Banbury Unitarian Fellowship, Banbury Town Hall.

18 St John the Evangelist RC Church, South Bar.

19 St Joseph the Worker RC Church, Edmunds Road, Banbury.

20 Southam Road Evangelical Church, corner of Cope Road in Southam Road.

21 Salvation Army, George Street.

22 Banbury and District Christian Spiritualist Church, Workhouse Lane, Bloxham.

23 Redeemed Christian Church of God (Lighthouse Parish), Banbury Town Hall.

No doubt there are other meetings, like the strict Calvinists on Hanwell Heights, which are not advertised. It is time to examine some of these groups or movements which have not been covered in earlier chapters.

Unitarians[1]

The term Unitarian within the Christian tradition describes an adherent of the view that God is one, and that Jesus is subordinate, as opposed to the Trinitarian Christian who believes that God the Father, his son, Jesus, and the Holy Ghost are three equal persons within one godhead. There are two main difficulties in tracing the history of Unitarianism. In this country there was no central Unitarian organisation until 1928 when the General Assembly of Unitarian and Free Christian Churches was formed. The other difficulty lies within the nature of Unitarianism itself. There is no creed, and in the past it has been difficult to determine who claimed to be a Unitarian and who did not. The modern establishment of Unitarianism can be dated from the Great Ejection of 1662. The radical non-Tractarian elements of those who were ejected were chiefly among the Presbyterians. As we have seen in Chapter 5, a significant number of them joined the Congregationalists in the eighteenth century. However, by 1830 most of the remaining Presbyterians, and many Baptists and Independents, had 'succumbed to the temptations of

Unitarianism'.[2] For most of the nineteenth century, the Unitarians were ably led by the academic and philosophical James Martineau (1805-1900).

In Banbury and elsewhere it tended to be the elite in society, like the Cobb family, who were attracted to Unitarian theology. The Banbury Academy, a Presbyterian (later Unitarian) school, was founded by Peter Usher at the meeting-house off Horsefair and lasted until 1908. There was also the Unitarian Sunday School, founded in 1802, which was the oldest in Banbury and much favoured by the town's elite. It seems unlikely that Unitarian theology had much impact in the local villages. Currently the Unitarian congregation in Banbury has no church building but meets once monthly for worship at a room in the Town Hall. In Oxford the congregation meets at Harris Manchester College, which was completed in 1891. The magnificent Victorian chapel is adorned with a complete set of stained glass windows by William Morris and Edward Burne Jones, all of which depict traditional Unitarian themes.

Salvation Army

William Booth (1829-1912) was the founder of the Salvation Army. He was born near Nottingham into the Church of England but in 1844 he was converted by the Methodist revival. In 1854 he was persuaded by his masterful future wife, Catherine, to join the Methodist New Connexion. He became a travelling evangelist for them and began to gather celebrity as a revivalist preacher. His wife's gifts were as powerful as those of her husband. This astonishing woman, who brought up eight children in uncomfortable accommodation, led revivals all over the country. They both knew that evangelism, revival, not a steady ministry to a chapel or circuit, was their vocation. When the Methodist Conference of 1861 refused Booth leave to become a travelling evangelist, he resigned and drifted out of the Connexion. Like Charles Spurgeon, the Baptist, he began to preach in the open, in parks or on street corners. In 1865, he came to London and with others formed the evangelical Christian Revival Association.

At the annual meeting of August 1878, which was called Our War Congress, the name was changed to The Salvation Army, a battle song was adopted and the evangelists began to be called field officers. In October 1879 Booth was called for the first time the General of the Salvation Army or simply 'the General' to his colleagues. From the beginning the Army gave equal status to its women workers and by 1878 forty-one of the Army's ninety-one officers were women. All Salvationists are expected to be total abstainers, and officers are expected to be non-smokers. Much of the Army's work has been among the most deprived section of the community and it is justly renowned for its provision of hostels for the homeless. These people were 'the vice of the slums' and none of the other religious groups could get down to them. If the Army could, they deserved a blessing. There was a detached respect from educated men for the Army's methods in the cities, much the same as there was for the Primitive Methodists in the villages. Indeed, the Army seems to have had a natural link with the Primitive Methodists. As their fortunes declined, many of them became Salvationists. In Deddington, for example, the old Bethel (the common name for a Primitive Methodist chapel) on the High Street became the Salvation Army barracks in 1898.

In Banbury, the Salvation officers began to hold services in the Central Corn Exchange in May 1880. As in other towns, the Army provoked uproar by accusing other Christians of wanting 'order, eloquence and respectability' in their chapels rather than souls, and asserting (correctly) that half the town's population never went to a place of worship. They established a permanent presence at the new Citadel on George Street in 1888. Among those with their name on a foundation stone is 'Holy Joe' John Griffin from Horley. He was an active member of the Army, a farmer and horse dealer, and he ran Temperance meetings at The Happy Hour Meeting Room in Horley in the 1890s. He was also quarrelsome and never stopped talking. After he died, railings were put round his grave and it was said that 'you needed to jump on his grave to keep him in'!

Today, the Salvation Army is a worldwide Christian Church working in 124 countries, with some 50,000 members in the UK. It is all a tribute to the visionary William Booth, who by the time of his death in 1912 had been received by King Edward VII at Buckingham Palace in 1904, given the freedom of the City of London in 1905, and in 1907 made an honorary doctor of laws by Oxford University. This was remarkable progress for the former ranting street evangelist and a clear acceptance of the role of the Army. Locally, the Banbury Corps, based at the Citadel in George Street, continues with an active programme of worship and community work.

Temperance[3]

The Temperance movement in Banbury was started in 1834 by Samuel Beesley, the well-known Quaker, confectioner and Liberal. The new Temperance Society quickly flourished and in the 1840s a Temperance hotel was opened, a meeting-room was fitted up in Parson's Street, and a ladies association was formed. In 1844, a Rechabite 'tent', a teetotal friendly society, was formed and its first festival was modelled closely on the traditional Club

Day celebrations, which were celebrated in most villages. By 1844 there was also a Teetotal Brass Band. The Temperance movement was particularly strong in the late nineteenth century, as people began to realise the seriousness of the drink problem. The Banbury Temperance Guild was still meeting in 1949, with numerous societies involved, including the Methodists, Templars, Rechabites, Quakers, Baptists and the Salvation Army.

In the eighteenth and early nineteenth centuries, Deddington was celebrated for the consumption of its 'malt-liquor', earning it the epithet of 'Drunken Deddington'. It was also said that its people proverbially 'sold the bells to buy drink'. In the late nineteenth century, however, they formed branches of the Rechabites and the Church of England Temperance Society, together with a Temperance Benefit Society. In so doing, they transformed the town into 'as sober and self-respecting a community as any in Oxfordshire'.[4] It is relevant to note the link between the Dissenters and Temperance. The Deddington Methodists joined the Wesleyan Reformers in 1850 and in 1857 there were said to be some 1,000 Dissenters in the town, about half the population. Even in 1895 there were still two Methodist preachers and six auxiliaries in the parish. This does not mean that all Methodists were committed to temperance, although the Primitive Methodists in particular, along with the Quakers, campaigned for it. In Fritwell, as we have seen, there was a similar link between the Dissenters and temperance, and in 1892 the new Wesleyan Reform chapel was also described as the Temperance Hall. That said, the King's Arms was run for a time by John Tebby, a Methodist. In the late nineteenth century, Temperance societies also organised numerous events for families, in places like Kirtlington Park and Shelswell Park. Like the Methodists, they were keen to be involved in all aspects of people's lives.

Plymouth Brethren (The Brethren)

The Brethren first met in Dublin about 1827. The first assembly in England was in Plymouth in December 1831, hence the name, and by 1845 some 1,000 were meeting there. They had established a meeting in Banbury by 1857, when they were assembling in the Temperance Hall on Parson's Street. John Poulton, a cabinet maker, left the Congregationalists to join them sometime after 1853. By the early 1860s they were meeting in the former Congregationalist chapel in Church Passage. The Brethren have been in decline in the UK since the 1950s and I have not found any current record of a meeting, although there are still likely to be some small groups meeting in people's houses. The Brethren have no hierarchy, no clergy, no creed, no liturgy and no register of members. They avoid symbols and do not display a cross anywhere. They prefer a bare room and their sole authority is the Bible. Like the Quakers they hold meetings not services. Their leadership and teaching is generally reserved to men, following their interpretation of the Bible.

Latter-Day Saints (Mormons)

The Church of the Latter-Day Saints was founded in 1830 in the USA and popularised by Brigham Young. The sect, after a controversial existence, settled in Salt Lake City, Utah, where it remains to this day. A feature of the Church is its encouragement of members to discover their ancestors, so that they might be posthumously admitted to membership. Hence, its extensive funding of the study of genealogy and exceptional computerised family records. There seem to have been very few members locally in the nineteenth century and most Banburians who joined them chose to go to America rather than stay to form a meeting in the town.[5] However, there is a reference to some Mormons in Eydon c.1850. More recently, a Mormon group has been meeting in Banbury on the corner of Chatsworth Drive and Bankside for some twenty-five years.

Witchcraft

The witch and witchcraft is mainly a story of the sixteenth and seventeenth centuries, in particular the mid-seventeenth century, when Matthew Hopkins, the Norfolk 'witch-finder', was on the prowl. It would therefore seem to have little to do with Nonconformity. However, ancient superstitions and folklore survived long afterwards, particularly in the more remote village communities, which were also natural homes for Nonconformity. The last Witchcraft Statute was repealed in 1736 but the authorities still used it in 1944 to secure the 'Last Witch Conviction'. In 1875 George Dew of Lower Heyford reported that: Ann Tustin died 'widely regarded as a witch'. She was given 'rough music', also known as 'skimmington' or 'lewbelling' i.e. 'lewd-belling' treatment.[6] This was the treatment for cuckolds or wife beating, as was the burning of effigies of the couple. Even in 1949, there was the following comment about Tysoe: 'At the beginning of the 20th century a strong belief in witchcraft prevailed here, cases of assault to draw blood from a suspected witch occurring, and aged women being reluctant to use the aid of a walking-stick, as that was a notorious sign of a witch. This is perhaps not unsuitable for a village which derived its name from the heathen god, Tiw'.[7] Even today there are still occasional headlines about witchcraft in the United Kingdom and children abused or killed for being evil and bewitched.

Chapter 10

Conclusion

IN THIS OVERVIEW, we have looked at the history and beliefs of the great variety of Nonconformists in Banburyshire. We have seen their strength and influence in the local communities and how, over the centuries, they have succeeded against all the odds in establishing their meetings and building their chapels and meeting-houses. In particular, we have seen how the Methodists have dominated the Nonconformist scene in the region, notably in the nineteenth century. It was my vivid childhood memories of John Bunyan's *Pilgrim's Progress* and his hobgoblin which inspired me to go back to the time of his persecution and imprisonment. How fortunate that my plans coincided with the 350th anniversary of the Great Ejection of ministers in 1662 and the origins of English Nonconformity; also with the great service of commemoration in Westminster Abbey on 7 February 2012. Apart from Bunyan himself, this period of Nonconformity has seen some towering figures, including Fox of the Quakers, Wesley of the Methodists, Spurgeon of the Baptists and Newman of the Catholics. It has been fascinating to look at them and their achievements and the inspiration which they brought to their followers. At the same time, it has been an opportunity to acknowledge and admire the achievements of these followers. We have seen numerous examples of their persistence and commitment, even courage, in founding the local meetings and, in most cases, building a chapel or meeting-house.

It has been a privilege for me to meet a variety of these committed followers: Methodists, Quakers, Baptists, Catholics and others. It is not an easy life for them in a time of falling congregations and financial problems. They also have to contend with an increasing number of secularists and atheists, who seem more notable for what they oppose, namely all faiths and what they call 'some of the more destructive religious impulses', than for anything positive. But, as someone wrote recently, 'How are these secularists so sure of what is out there, and are there not some things which are 'beyond reason?' It must be said that the weakness of the Church of England over the last fifty years, albeit in a time of huge changes in our society, has given the secularists their opportunity. We have seen how a similar weakness of the Church in the late eighteenth and early nineteenth centuries allowed the various strands of Dissent to prosper. But we have also seen just how different society was in the nineteenth century and how religion permeated every aspect of many people's lives; we have noted this particularly in local Methodist communities. Sadly, this is not the case today, many rural chapels have closed, and this trend seems likely to continue.

I have certainly found researching this study an inspirational experience and enjoyed the warmth of the welcome and support which I have received from Nonconformists of various persuasions. I think that I can now understand better the comfort and support which they and not the Church of England can often provide. Who is to say that these Nonconformists may not continue to provide it for their members, even if the odds do seem stacked against them by the 'secularist surge'? I should finish where I started, some 350 years ago, with John Bunyan's *Pilgrim's Progress*, the simple, yet unique, allegory written during his twelve years in gaol; also with the sublime beauty of the Holy Trinity Chapel at Staunton Harold, for which Sir Robert Shirley died as a prisoner in the Tower. Like these two remarkable pilgrims, from their different worlds, I hope that any future pilgrims may be able to say with them that 'hobgoblin nor foul fiend could daunt his spirit'.

Appendix

Letter from John Henry Newman, Banbury Guardian, 3 July 1862.

A LETTER FROM MR. NEWMAN.

The following letter from Mr. John Henry Newman was published in the *Globe* of Monday :—

To the Editor of the *Globe*.

Sir,—A friend has sent me word of a paragraph about me which appeared in your paper of yesterday, to the effect that "I have left, or am about to leave, my Oratory at Brompton, of which I have been for several years the head, as a preliminary, in the expectation of my private friends, to my return to the Church of England."

I consider that you have transferred this statement into your columns from those of a contemporary in order to give me the opportunity of denying it, if I am able to do so. Accordingly I lose not an hour in addressing these lines to you. which I shall be obliged by your giving at once to the public.

The paragraph is utterly unfounded in every portion of it.

1. For the last 13 years I have been head of the Birmingham Oratory. I am head still ; and I have no reason to suppose that I shall cease to be head unless advancing years should incapacitate me for the duties of my station.

2. On the other hand, from the time that I founded the London Oratory, now at Brompton, 12 years ago, I have had no jurisdiction over it whatever ; and so far from being its head, it so happens I have not been within its walls for the last seven years.

3. I have not had one moment's wavering of trust in the Catholic Church ever since I was received into her fold. I hold, and ever have held, that her Sovereign Pontiff is the centre of unity and the Vicar of Christ ; and I ever have had, and have still, an unclouded faith in her creed in all its articles ; a supreme satisfaction in her worship, discipline, and teaching ; and an eager longing and a hope against hope that the many dear friends whom I have left in Protestantism may be partakers of my happiness.

4. This being my state of mind, to add, as I hereby go on to do, that I have no intention, and never have had any intention, of leaving the Catholic Church, and becoming a Protestant again, would be superfluous, except that Protestants are always on the look out for some loophole or evasion in a Catholic's statement of fact. Therefore, in order to give them full satisfaction, if I can, I do hereby profess *ex animo*, with an absolute internal assent and consent, that Protestanism is the dreariest of possible religions ; that the thought of the Anglican services makes me shiver, and the thought of the Thirty-nine Articles makes me shudder. Return to the Church of England ! No : "the net is broken, and we are delivered." I should be a consummate fool (to use a mild term) if in my old age I left "the land flowing with milk and honey" for the city of confusion and the house of bondage.—I am, Sir, your obedient servant,

JOHN H. NEWMAN.

The Oratory, Birmingham, June 28.

Notes

Foreword and Acknowledgements

1 Michael Watts, *The Dissenters*, 220.
2 Preface to *The Pilgrim's Progress*, vii (Hendrickson Christian Classics)
3 Christopher Hill, *A Tinker and a Poor Man*, 175.

Introduction: Why Banburyshire?

1 Barrie Trinder, *Victorian Banbury*, 16.
2 Brian Little, *Banbury – A History*, 1.
3 *Banbury Guardian*, 6 July, 1843, quoted by Barrie Trinder, 16.
4 Martin Blinkhorn in Preface to *The Pathways of Banburyshire* by E.Walford (1900, revised 1983).

Chapter 1: Old Dissent

1 For this paragraph I am indebted to Richard Ollard, *This War without an Enemy*, 208-9.
2 *Archaeological Journal*, Vol 112 (1956), 173.
3 John Morrill (ed), *The Impact of the Civil War* (1991), 117.
4 For this and the following section I am indebted to Michael Watts, *The Dissenters*.
5 Watts, *The Dissenters*, 194.
6 A.G.Matthews, *Calamy Revised*, Introduction, xii-xiv.
7 Watts, 220.
8 Mary Clapinson,(ed), *Bishop Fell and Nonconformity*, 1682-83, Introduction, xxvi.
9 Watts, 247.
10 Preface to *The Pilgrim's Progress*, vii.
11 Watts, 261.
12 Watts, 270.
13 Watts, 385.
14 Watts, 509.
15 Michael R.Watts, *The Chapel and the Nation*, 5.

The 1851 Religious Census

1 W.T.Henderson, *Recollections of his Life*, Vol 2, 114-5.
2 For the Oxfordshire figures, see Kate Tiller, *Church and Chapel in Oxfordshire 1851*, xxxiv.

Chapter 3: Methodists (New Dissent)

1 Flora Thompson, *Lark Rise to Candleford*, 219.
2 Public Record Office, RG4 2021; I am indebted to Patricia List for bringing this to my attention.
3 Clyde Binfield, *So Down to Prayers*, 5.
4 Watts, *The Chapel and the Nation*, 26.
5 Owen Chadwick, *The Victorian Church*, Part One, 375.
6 Chadwick, Part One, 381.
7 Watts, *The Chapel*, 26.
8 Chadwick, Part One, 386.
9 Barrie Tabraham, *The Making of Methodism* (1995).
10 Chadwick, Part Two, 281.
11 This section owes much to my *Parishes, Parsons and Persuasions* (1997).
12 *Kelly's Directory,* Oxon, 1864.
13 J.C.Blomfield, *Fritwell*.
14 E.P.Baker (ed), *Bishop Wilberforce's Visitation Returns for the Archdeaconry of Oxford* (1854).
15 *Bicester Herald*, 17 April 1874.
16 *Bicester Herald*, 22 May 1874.
17 MS.Oxf.Dioc. c.344.
18 David Newsome, *The Victorian World Picture*, 74-5.
19 Clyde Binfield, *So Down to Prayers*, xi.
20 Binfield, 9.
21 Pamela Horn (ed.), *The Early Diaries of George James Dew*, 67.
22 *Lark Rise*, 219.
23 A.Hume, *Remarks on the Census of Religious Worship for England and Wales* (1860), 17, quoted by Kate Tiller, xxix.
24 W.T.Henderson, *Recollections of his Life*, Vol 2, 115.
25 Chadwick, Part Two, 159.
26 *Bicester Herald*, 5 June 1865.
27 Newsome, 74-5.
28 Oxford Diocesan Papers, d.179 and d.332.
29 Ralph Mann, *Wigginton Methodist Chapel, 1883-2008*, 9.
30 *Banbury Advertiser*, 31 May 1900.

Chapter 4: Baptists

1 Trinder, 111.
2 Trinder, 5.
3 Chadwick, Part One, 419-20.

4   Chadwick, Part One, 417-8.
5   Christopher Howse, quoted in Daily Telegraph, 29 October 1998.
6   W.T. Henderson, Vol 2, 114-5.
7   For this paragraph I am indebted to the Nomenclature Board of Tasmania.
8   The 1851 Religious Census for Moreton Pinkney, Northamptonshire, 71.
9   Syd Tyrrell, *A Countryman's Tale*, 93.
10 Ralph Mann, *Wigginton Methodist Chapel*, 3.

Chapter 5: Congregationalists/Independents

1   Trinder, 42.
2   Archbishop Rowan Williams, in his sermon at Westminster Abbey, 7 February 2012.

Chapter 6: The Society of Friends (Quakers)

1   Watts, *The Dissenters*, 193.
2   Pauline Ashridge, *Children of Dissent,* 35.
3   Jack V.Wood, *Some Rural Quakers*, 12.
4   Watts, 385.
5   Watts, 385-90.
6   Watts, 461.
7   Binfield, 5-7.
8   For this note I am indebted to Nick Allen.
9   Christopher Stell, *Nonconformist Chapels and Meeting-houses.*

Chapter 7: Roman Catholics

1   *Lark Rise*, 213-4.
2   *Lark Rise*, 213-4.
3   *Lark Rise*, 471-2.
4   For this note I am indebted to Philip Suffolk, *Catholic Brailes, Some Notes on its History* (undated).

Chapter 8: Chapel and Community

1   Chadwick, Part Two, 112 and 159.
2   Newsome, 65.
3   Newsome, 65-6.
4   Newsome, 66; *Lark Rise*, 470-2.

5   Watts, *The Chapel*, 23.

6   Watts, *The Chapel*, 30.

7   Chadwick, Part Two, 112 and 159

8   J.H. Bettey, *Church and Community, The Parish Church in English Life*, 129 (1979)

9   M.K.Ashby, *Joseph Ashby of Tysoe*, 77 (1961)

10 V.C.H. *Oxon*. vi, 115 (Ploughley Hundred).

11 Syd Tyrrell, *A Countryman's Tale*, 102.

12 Mary Ingrams, Portrait of a Village, *Focus Magazine* (1978).

Chapter 9: Other Groups and Movements

1   For this paragraph I am indebted to Gavin Lloyd.

2   Archbishop Rowan Williams, in his sermon at Westminster Abbey on 7 February 2012.

3   Trinder, 71-2.

4   H.M.Colvin, *History of Deddington*, 77-9, slightly expanded by Christopher Day.

5   Trinder, 114.

6   Pamela Horn (ed.), *The Early Diaries of George James Dew*, 59.

7   V.C.H. *Warwickshire*, v (Kineton Hundred).

Bibliography

For those who may wish to explore the history of Nonconformity further, I attach a list of the main primary and published sources which I have consulted.

Primary Sources

John Bunyan, *The Pilgrim's Progress* (1678/1684).
Methodist Records, including Circuit and Preacher Plans.
Religious Census of 1851.
Trade directories, including *Rusher's Lists*.

Published Sources

M.K.Ashby, *Joseph Ashby of Tysoe, A Study of English Village Life* (1961).
Pauline Ashbridge, *Children of Dissent* (2008).
Leslie Baily, *From the Romans to Rock-N-Roll: A Short History of the Sibford-Epwell-Hook Norton-District* (1960).
Trevor Beeson, *Round the Church in 50 Years, An intimate journey* (2007).
Clyde Binfield, *So Down to Prayers: Studies in English Nonconformity, 1780-1920* (1977).
Owen Chadwick, *The Victorian Church, Part One, 1829-1859* (1966); *Part Two, 1860-1901* (1966).
Mary Clapinson (editor), *Bishop Fell and Nonconformity: Visitation Documents from the Oxford Diocese, 1682-83* (Oxfordshire Record Society 52, 1980).
Martin Greenwood, *Parishes, Parsons and Persuasions: the contrasting clerics and communities of Fringford and Fritwell in 19th-century North Oxfordshire* (1997, not published).
Martin Greenwood, *Villages of Banburyshire, including Lark Rise to Candleford Green* (Wychwood Press, 2006).
Martin Greenwood, *In Flora's Footsteps, Daily Life in Lark Rise Country, 1876-2009* (Wychwood Press, 2009).
Brian Little, *Banbury – A History* (2003).
David Newsome, *The Victorian World Picture* (1997).
Walter Stageman, *Closed Places of Worship in South Northamptonshire* (Northamptonshire Association for Local History, Hindsight Issue 17, 2011).
Christopher Stell, *Nonconformist Chapels and Meeting-Houses, Northamptonshire & Oxfordshire* (1986).

David Thompson, *Nonconformity in the Nineteenth Century* (1972).

Flora Thompson, *Lark Rise to Candleford* (1945).

Barrie Trinder, *Victorian Banbury* (1982).

Syd Tyrrell, *A Countryman's Tale* (1973).

Syd Tyrell's Eydon (Eydon Historical Research Group, 2001).

Victoria County History, vi (Ploughley Hundred), 1959; ix (Bloxham Hundred), 1969; x (Banbury Hundred), 1972; xi (Wootton Hundred (Northern Part)), 1983.

Michael Watts, *The Dissenters, From the Reformation to the French Revolution* (1978).

Michael R.Watts, *The Chapel and the Nation, Nonconformity and The Local Historian* (1996).

Chapter 1 Old Dissent

Christopher Hill, *A Tinker and a Poor Man, John Bunyan and His Church, 1628-1688* (1988).

A.G.Matthews, *Calamy Revised* (1934).

Alan B.F.Sell (ed.) *The Great Ejectment of 1662, Its Antecedents, Aftermath, and Ecumenical Significance* (2012).

John H.Taylor (ed.), *1662 and Its Issues* (Congregational Historical Society, April 1962).

Chapter 2: The 1851 Religious Census

Edward Legg (ed.), *Buckinghamshire Returns of the Census of Religious Worship 1851* (1991).

Kate Tiller (ed.), *Church and Chapel in Oxfordshire 1851: The return of the census of religious worship*, Oxfordshire Record Society 55 (1987).

Graham S.Ward (ed.), *The 1851 Religious Census of Northamptonshire* (2007).

Chapter 3: Methodists (New Dissent)

Pauline Ashbridge, *Village Chapels* (2004).

David Gill, *The Kineton Methodists, 1842-1993* (1994).

Cheryl Gilkes, *Methodism in the Banbury Circuit, 1784-1932* (1973, not published).

Ralph Mann, *Wigginton Methodist Chapel, 1883-2008: 125 years* (2008).

Audrey Martin, *The Changing Faces of the Bartons* (The Bartons History Group, 1999).

Geoffrey Milburn, *Primitive Methodism* (Epworth Press, 2002).

T.J.Rigg, *Jottings of Hinton Methodism* (2002).

T.J.Rigg, *Balscote Methodism 1850-2000*.

Kate Tiller, 'The desert begins to blossom': Oxfordshire and the Primitive Methodists, 1824-1860' (*Oxoniensia* LXXI p.85-109, 2006).

Barrie Trinder, *The Methodist Church, Marlborough Road, Banbury, Centenary Celebrations of Present Church* (1965).

John Munsey Turner, *John Wesley: The Evangelical Revival and the Rise of Methodism in England* (Epworth Press, 2002).

John Munsey Turner, *Wesleyan Methodism* (Epworth Press, 2005).

Chapter 4: Baptists

Ruth Barbour, *W.T.Henderson (1825-1911): a radical Baptist minister* (Open University Project, undated).

C.H.Spurgeon, *The Metropolitan Tabernacle, Its History and Work* (republished 1990).

Rev'd Paul Taylor et al, *A History of Hook Norton Baptist Church* (2010).

Chapter 6: The Society of Friends (Quakers)

Nicholas Allen, 'The Doylys of Adderbury and their Quaker Meeting House' (*Cake and Cock Horse*, Spring 2012).

Jack V.Wood, *Some Rural Quakers* (1991).

Chapter 7: Catholics

Joy Grant, *Hethe-with-Adderbury, The story of a Catholic parish in Oxfordshire* (2000).

Index